THE LIFE AND TIMES
OF THE
STATION MASTER

Spotlight on

Broadbottom

Broadbottom, a former L & N E R station, is situated 9¾ miles along the electrified line from Manchester to Sheffield (Victoria). It serves the villages of Broadbottom, Mottram and Charlesworth and has, in the main, residential passenger traffic.

Some 400 yds inside the boundary of Cheshire, marked by the River Etherow, Broadbottom in the summertime is the starting point for ramblers, hikers and rock-climbers setting out for a day in the nearby Derbyshire beauty spots. From the platforms there is a wonderful view of the Longendale valley.

The station buildings, constructed by the Sheffield, Ashton-under-Lyne & Manchester Railway for £500, according to local historical records, consist of solid Derbyshire stone. They are considered to be of such architectural beauty that they have not been affected in any way by subsequent building.

Each July the station is used as an official "clock setting" point, when time recording clocks for the famous Rheims (France) to England homing pigeon race are sent to Broadbottom from places all over the North of England for official synchronisation.

Pictured in our photo strip are Stationmaster Arnold Young; Clerk Leslie England; Sub-Ganger Cyril Coverley and Jnr Porter Norman Teasdale.

THE LIFE AND TIMES OF THE STATION MASTER

DAVID HOLMES

· RAILWAY HERITAGE ·
from
The NOSTALGIA Collection

To my wife Jan and daughter Diana for their help and encouragement

First published in 2007

British Library Cataloguing in Publication Data

A catalogue record for this book is available from the British Library.

ISBN 978 1 85794 282 8

Silver Link Publishing Ltd
The Trundle
Ringstead Road
Great Addington
Kettering
Northants NN14 4BW

Tel/Fax: 01536 330588
email: sales@nostalgiacollection.com
Website: www.nostalgiacollection.com

Printed and bound in Great Britain

All photographs are by the author unless otherwise credited.
Items of ephemera and paperwork credited 'WA' are from the collection of Will Adams.

Half title Master of all he surveys: Norton station on the Birkenhead Joint line in Cheshire just before the First World War. *John Ryan collection*

Frontispiece The old order: the Station Master and members of his staff at Broadbottom as featured in *British Railways London Midland Magazine* of May 1962. *WA*

Title page The office and platform staff at Bowling Junction, Bradford, are justly proud of the appearance of their station. *John Ryan collection*

BIBLIOGRAPHY

Chapman, Stephen and Rose, Peter *Railway Memories No 6: Ardsley, Wakefield and Normanton* (Bellcode Books, 1994)

MacDermot, E. T. *History of the Great Western Railway: Volume 1 1833-1863* (Great Western Railway Company, 1927)

Richards, Jeffrey and MacKenzie, John M. *The Railway Station: A social history* (Oxford University Press, 1986)

Simmons, Jack and Biddle, Gordon *The Oxford Companion to British Railway History* (Oxford University Press, 1997)

White, Malcolm R. *The Yarmouth Train* (Malcolm R. White, Coastal Publications, 2005)

My thanks to the staff at Steam: Museum of the Great Western Railway, Swindon, for their assistance.

CONTENTS

No 42073 stands at Castleford Central station with the 2.30pm Pontefract Baghill-Leeds Central service on 3 April 1961. This was about seven years before the author took over as Station Master and nine years before the job title disappeared for ever.

INTRODUCTION

It was in the early 1970s that the old job title of Station Master (SM), together with Yard Master and Shed Master, disappeared. In some parts of the country the designation of SM had already gone by then, but it lingered on for a few years in what had been the North Eastern Region of British Rail. The word 'Master' really did belong to the 19th century.

On today's railways many stations are unmanned, with just 'bus-stop'-type shelters. It is very important, of course, that such stations continue to provide an increasingly frequent and reliable service in these days of appalling congestion on the roads. Larger towns and cities still have manned stations, with people doing essentially the same type of work as in the past but under more modern names.

In the chapters that follow we will see how the old job of SM varied according to the size of the station, the number of staff and the mix of traffic – passenger, goods and parcels – as well as 'operating', a word little used nowadays. In fact, the first line of responsibility for many SMs was to the District Operating Superintendent, because of the importance of Safety of the Line duties, of which 'Rules & Regs', as they were known, were an essential part.

As with other jobs on the railways or elsewhere there are three levels of organisation to consider. The SM was on the middle level, reporting to the District or Divisional Office, which was not just there to supervise but also to provide important services and support to enable the SM to do his job. Then the SM himself had staff to do the work 24 hours a day, seven days a week. Managing such staff, and with so many safety considerations, made the SM's job important and very satisfying. It helped if you were a railway enthusiast but, to many, it was just a job like any other.

It is a strange coincidence that the designation of SM disappeared at about the same time as the end of steam on Britain's railways, but it gives me a perfect excuse to illustrate this book with steam-era photos and memorabilia. We will look at what an SM did and, hopefully, reach an understanding of the importance of the job on the old railway that was so dear to so many people; thankfully the work is continued by today's railwaymen and, increasingly, women.

The traditional country station as it appears in films such as *The Titfield Thunderbolt*, with SM, booking clerk, porter, and signal box with semaphore signals, was hard to find even many years ago, and it is no coincidence that preserved lines make a point of having such stations to visit as well as steam trains

Fairford was an idyllic country branch line terminus and probably what most people would regard as the ideal station for an SM to carry out his duties. Sadly this station and the Fairford branch closed to passengers just over six weeks after this photograph was taken, at 11.45am on 2 May 1962, with the 12.12am train to Oxford awaiting departure behind 0-6-0 No 2221. In 1906 the branch was notable for what the GWR *Magazine* described as the new audible signal arrangement, which was experimentally installed in place of semaphore Distant signals following trials in the London area. All 14 Distant signals were removed and replaced by Audible Signal ramps between the rails; these electro-mechanical devices activated a signal inside the cab – a bell for All Right and a steam whistle for Danger.

to attract the casual visitor and the enthusiast. I don't remember actually seeing the SM in the film, but you knew that he was there. Indeed, his presence on screen would have stopped some of the more dubious practices and spoiled the film! All good fun, of course, but fortunately pure fiction. However, it was a lovely reminder of sun-filled days, steam trains and the porter with time to spare between trains to tend the station gardens.

In real life the SM had a vital role, whether it was at the traditional quaint old station on a branch line, a medium-sized station in a colliery area or the ultimate, the man wearing the top hat – on auspicious occasions – at King's Cross.

In addition to the more formal duties, I feel that the job encapsulated the true spirit and essence of the railway world so important to all who have an interest in railways, both as they were in steam days and today. I shall illustrate this by

recounting some interesting and relevant experiences from my own period as an SM between 1962 at East Leake and 1970 at Castleford. The SM was part of a large railway family, and you dealt with drivers, guards and many other staff as well as your own, often for extended hours when On Call. The essential thing was to keep the trains moving safely and punctually and deal with any problems that occurred.

But first let us examine how the post of Station Master evolved over the years.

EARLY DAYS

In the early days of the railways the title of SM was not in use. There was instead an employee known as a Policeman, who had an amazing variety of duties of which signalling, in its earliest and most primitive form, was probably the most important. This became, of course, the work later performed by signalmen. The

The station garden was an important feature of many stations in more leisured times when there was sufficient manpower to tend them. In the first view the SM himself (left) has joined his staff and taken spade in hand to deal with the spring flowers at Heald Green on the LNWR near Stockport, while in the other the SM and a young admirer pose with a vast display of blooms on the platform at Pennington, Lancashire. *Both John Ryan collection*

Policemen's work was mainly an outside, on-the-line sort of job. Within the station was another person with the designation of Station Clerk, Agent or even, at large stations, Superintendent. His duties included inspecting the station buildings, and checking the use of stores, stationery, coal, gas and oil. A very important duty was to check the appearance of staff and their behaviour towards passengers. He also decided the order and timely despatch of trains. However, at some small stations the Policemen would be in sole charge.

An Act of 1835 stated that the officer in charge of a station must have his Christian name and surname painted on a board above the booking office door as he was the collector of rates and tolls.

The Great Western Railway (GWR) officially adopted the 'Station Master' title in about 1860, but Station Clerks had become known unofficially as Station Masters for quite some time before that, and at one time had goods as well as passenger station responsibilities. On the same railway the Superintendent of the Line ran the department that covered passenger and operating, while goods was a separate department, as were the engineering and locomotive departments. In many parts of the country the titles Station Master, Ticket Collector and Porter were in regular use as early as 1849. Until 1865 SMs on the GWR wore plain clothes and a top hat, and in the 1860s an SM at a small station was paid about £80 per annum. At larger stations the annual remuneration rose to about £200, with about £100 being the overall average. Many SMs worked their way up from porter or clerk at that time.

The SM was an important local figure alongside the doctor and the vicar. He canvassed for traffic and so became well known to the local business community.

In 1910 in Britain 621,340 people worked for the railways, of whom 169,572 worked at stations, 8,688 being SMs. Eventually no fewer than one million people were employed by the railways. In 1935 the GWR had 747 SMs.

THE 1950S AND '60S

In the 1950s and '60s the diversity of an SM's work was large taking into consideration the number of staff and traffics dealt with. My first SM job, at East Leake on the former Great Central Railway (GCR) main line to London, with eight staff – on paper, anyway – was obviously very different from that at King's Cross. My eight people covered operating duties (signalmen), freight, passenger and parcels work. The freight revenue was several times greater than that of passenger traffic. Later, when I was SM at Elland (on the former Lancashire & Yorkshire line between Halifax and Dewsbury), the two passenger stations (the other being Greetland) were closed, but there was a power station with several trains each day. From this it can be seen that even smaller stations varied a good deal – it could almost be said that no two were alike.

At larger stations there were often separate Passenger and Parcels Agents as well as an SM; this was the case, for example, at two stations with which I was involved during a period of Management Training, at Hull Paragon and Newcastle Central.

Many years ago there was no choice of where you started your railway career, or even in which department. You were invited to take promotion if considered suitable. In some railway jobs people were just sent to where they were required. In the case of an SM there would usually be a station house, perhaps rent-free or with a subsidised rent, which you were obliged to occupy. Other staff were not so fortunate, however.

So what was the purpose of the job of

Above In 1964 the SM at Horsforth was also in charge of Headingley station, on the former NER Leeds-Harrogate line. The station buildings with booking office and fire-buckets are on the right, with the northbound platform behind the photographer. There were also coal drops and a small goods yard here, and lower-quadrant signals and gas lamps were still in use at this time. 'V2' No 60940 passes through with the 5.37pm (SO) Manchester-Newcastle train on 17 June 1961.

Below Wigan North Western was a typical medium-sized West Coast Main Line station in the mid-1950s, and the SM at such a station would be present on the platform for the main trains. No 45545 *Planet* is arriving at 1.24pm with the 12.15pm Blackpool Central-Birmingham New Street service on 18 June 1955. There are many expectant passengers ready to board the train and also a barrow loaded with crates; note also the Refreshment Room and large station clock.

At one time most stations would have had their own SM. This is Thrapston Bridge Street at 1.18pm on 1 July 1963, with the 12.40pm Peterborough East-Northampton Castle train providing a cross-country stopping train serving towns and villages along the way. The Bradshaw timetable for 10 years earlier shows a similar train booked to call at Thrapston at 1.18pm.

Station Master, and where did it fit into the District, later Divisional, organisations? These questions will be explored in the following chapters, but regarding the question of why you wanted to be an SM, there are several answers. Maybe you had worked at a station and wished to be in charge of your own: it was a normal progression for many people in search of promotion from booking office clerk, signalman, operating clerk or District Inspector. Perhaps it was status and the possibility of eventually moving up to District Superintendent. Maybe you were a railway enthusiast and wanted to be out there dealing with the nitty-gritty of the railways.

As the 20th century progressed the Regional and District Offices took over more responsibilities and the SM became less important. Several stations would be put under one SM and eventually, in early February 1970, the job came to an end. I was in this situation as the last SM at Castleford when the Area Management organisation took over.

RELIEF SM

Finally in this brief introduction mention should be made of another essential job, that of Relief Station Master (RSM). If an SM was on leave, ill, on a course, or if the job was vacant, it was necessary to provide cover. It might be for only one day, which did not allow time to do very much, and in any case you did not wish to make changes to the way things were normally run. However, there could be problems to be solved and the normal On Call arrangements to cover. Relief Clerks had a similar sort of life; in fact, some RSMs, while being busy in the summer, would find themselves doing clerical jobs in the winter when there was less leave to cover. Some were pleased to do this, while others, perhaps getting on in years, would be happy to settle into a permanent office job after years of travelling about and maybe having to cover On Call for long periods and probably quite a long way from home in those days when few people had cars.

1
A STATION MASTER'S JOB

ADVERTISING OF STATION MASTER POSTS

At one time it was not the practice to openly advertise SM jobs and invite suitably qualified people to apply. In this chapter and the next we will look at what was the normal situation, covering the whole spectrum of SMs' work in the 1950s and '60s with a brief mention of some early 1970s Area Management items that were a continuation of SM-type duties. So far as the advertising of SMs' jobs was concerned, we shall see that agreed procedures were in place to ensure fair play and to give everyone a chance of advancement. As with all walks of life, it depended on how keen you were and what efforts you were prepared to make to achieve your career objectives.

On the railways this involved moving around the country, accepting the On Call duties and, as you advanced, facing the problems at large stations in more difficult locations. Some aspects of SM jobs were similar to the more onerous responsibilities taken on by Yard Masters and Shed Masters at larger, busier places.

Vacancy lists

Each BR Region published vacancy lists every week. One list described SM jobs that were vacant, together with clerical jobs up to a particular level. The other list contained higher-graded jobs, but you did not get to see it until you were at or approaching management level in the strict grading system. Jobs might be permanent or temporary; the latter could be for a variety of reasons, including possible doubts about the future of the station or maybe plans to merge the job with another. Sometimes SM jobs could be filled for fairly short periods rather than covering them using an RSM for several months. The station house, if there was one, would be mentioned, and whether it would be vacant. Sometimes the vacancy would be cancelled if it became obvious that the planned changes would soon take effect.

You could apply for jobs at a higher grade than your own, even missing out a grade. Sideways moves – applying for another job at your existing grade – was possible but not always popular because almost certainly you would be the senior applicant and therefore likely to get an interview – and why did you want to leave your present job in the same grade anyway?

Occasionally a cryptic message appeared saying that there was no suitable applicant from the Region where the job

Above The Station Master's house is well-placed in the centre of the site at Beeston Castle & Tarporley station. *John Ryan collection*

Below The author is appointed as temporary SM at Batley in 1967.

British Railways Eastern Region

City Station
Leeds 1
Leeds 31711   Extn. 416   E. Dalton   Divisional Manager

Mr. D. Holmes,
c/o Goods Agent,
LEEDS HUNSLET LANE

y/r
o/r   LC31/36/N.1421(t)   27 October 1967

Dear Mr. Holmes,

Vacancy N.1421(t)   List 36   Station Master
Class 1(t)   Batley

I am pleased to inform you that you have been selected for appointment to the above mentioned temporary post at your present salary, although it is realised that the position is only of a temporary nature and of short duration it is felt that Managerial experience can be gained by you whilst occupying this post.

Please arrange to transfer to your new duties on Monday, 6th November, 1967.

Yours sincerely,

G. MYERS,
Divisional Movements Manager,
Leeds

was advertised and it would thus be thrown open to the other Regions. It was on this basis that I achieved my first SM job, on the former Great Central Railway (GCR) main line. The future of the route was uncertain at the time, hence the lack of applicants. In addition the house was not available, but there were On Call duties; this effectively meant living in lodgings for several months. At one time this had been a normal way of life for many railway people but was not very attractive in the 1960s, nor were lodgings easy to find.

The grade of the job and the On Call commitments were described. If the job was shown as Station Master/Goods Agent it was an indication of a reasonably sized freight responsibility. The operating side of the job, ie being in charge of signalmen, train running and shunting, etc, was implicit in the title of SM.

Application forms

There was a standard application form on which you wrote your cv, although such a term was not used in those days. We shall see more later about how the Divisional Office dealt with the application forms

'British Railways Welcome You': part of BR booklet issued to new entrants in the early 1950s, and published by the Railway Executive. *Author's collection*

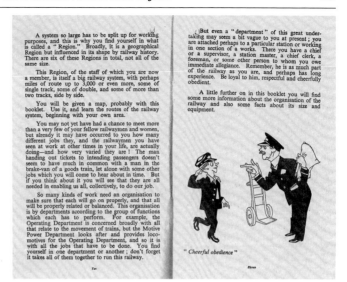

A system so large has to be split up for working purposes, and this is why you find yourself in what is called a "Region." Broadly, it is a geographical Region but influenced in its shape by railway history. There are six of these Regions in total, not all of the same size.

This Region, of the staff of which you are now a member, is itself a big railway system, with perhaps miles of route up to 3,000 or even more, some of single track, some of double, and some of more than two tracks, side by side.

You will be given a map, probably with this booklet. Use it, and learn the routes of the railway system, beginning with your own area.

You may not yet have had a chance to meet more than a very few of your fellow railwaymen and women, but already it may have occurred to you how many different jobs they, and the railwaymen you have seen at work at other times in your life, are actually doing—and how very varied they are! The man handing out tickets to intending passengers doesn't seem to have much in common with a man in the brake-van of a goods train, let alone with some other jobs which you will come to hear about in time. But if you think about it you will see that they are all needed in enabling us all, collectively, to do our job.

So many kinds of work need an organisation to make sure that each will go on properly, and that all will be properly related or balanced. This organisation is by departments according to the group of functions which each has to perform. For example, the Operating Department is concerned broadly with all that relate to the movement of trains, but the Motive Power Department looks after and provides locomotives for the Operating Department, and so it is with all the jobs that have to be done. You find yourself in one department or another; don't forget it takes all of them together to run this railway.

But even a "department" of this great undertaking may seem a bit vague to you at present; you are attached perhaps to a particular station or working in one section of a works. There you have a chief or a supervisor, a station master, a chief clerk, a foreman, or some other person to whom you owe immediate allegiance. Remember, he is as much part of the railway as you are, and perhaps has long experience. Be loyal to him, respectful and cheerfully obedient.

A little further on in this booklet you will find some more information about the organisation of the railway and also some facts about its size and equipment.

"Cheerful obedience"

and set up the subsequent interviews. The qualifications listed on the form would obviously play a part in deciding whether you were called in for interview and, together with previous experience, had a large bearing on whether you were successful.

In applying for your first SM post, much would depend on your background. If as a clerk you had booking office or operating clerk experience and had attended evening classes with good results, that would be a help. A signalman might not have any commercial background, but his obvious Safety of the Line – 'Rules & Regs' – knowledge was very important. Either way you would need to gain knowledge on the job in a lower-grade SM post, and an oral 'Block Exam', as it was known, was mandatory. This involved going through your knowledge of Rules & Regs with a District Signalmen's Inspector (DSI), to ensure that, from day one, you were competent in the vital safety elements of the job – safe train running, passenger and staff safety were paramount. I was lucky in that, as a booking clerk at one station, I had been able to spend every third Saturday afternoon in a signal box. It was strictly authorised, of course, and helped to give me a very good understanding of a signalman's duties.

Interviews

Usually the District Operating Superintendent (DOS) held the interviews, which emphasised again the importance of the operating and safety side of things. He would be your boss and there would, of course, be important links to the Passenger and Goods District Managers. A Staff (Personnel) man would also be present. Interviews could be difficult if the DOS was keen to ask questions about particular aspects of Rules & Regs – it was a very large subject! I can still remember my first day on the railway, as a Junior Clerk in 1954. I had an interview with the District Staff Manager and, fortunately, gave the correct answer to the question of what would be my main duty during my career with BR – it was service to the customers, both passenger and goods.

Grading system for SMs

The grading system for SMs from the early 1950s up to 1968 was an upside-down situation, Class 4 being the lowest grade, working up to Class 1, then Special A, Special B and Management grades. This was reversed in 1968 to make Class 1 the lowest. The grades of Railman, Leading Railman, etc, also commenced in 1968. Class 5 had disappeared in 1954 and there were few Class 4 SMs – Stretton & Clay Mills near Burton was one of the few that I remember. There was a time when SMs would move to an easier job approaching retirement. In a few cases an SM retiring at 65 would be annoyed to find that a young chap, perhaps from university, had taken over his job.

PROMOTION

Applying for promotion was on a similar basis to applying for your first SM position, except that you now had experience. If you were at a larger station you might be involved in doing some interviewing, and you were now asking the questions if, for instance, a clerical job at your station needed to be filled. I once sat in as an observer at an interview for apprenticeships at a large loco depot; one lad had travelled 10 miles by train and he was asked whether it was a steam, diesel or electric train. He had no idea and, although more questions followed, effectively the interview was over; if he had no interest in traction he would not be a suitable candidate. BR promoted from within except for some specialised jobs such as architects, where it was necessary to bring people in from outside industry, perhaps to a fairly highly graded job. Things have changed nowadays, of course.

Whatever the job, no matter how high or low, if you could demonstrate enthusiasm for railway work in general and had attended evening classes or helped gain new traffic you were in with a chance. Seniority did not count for as much as it did for the so-called 'wages grades' jobs, ie non-clerical or non-management posts.

PAY

In 1950 the lowest-grade SM – Class 6 – was paid £280 per annum. At that time an engine-driver's top weekly rate was 138 shillings (£6 18s), and for a signalman 127 shillings (£6 7s). Note the way in which pay rates were quoted: per annum for salaried staff and per week for wages grades. In 1960, when I was a booking clerk, my take-home pay after stoppages was about £7 a week plus sometimes a little overtime covering the porter's job. My pay as a Class 3 SM in 1962 was about £13 a week, after stoppages for tax, pension contribution and NHI. This was actually paid fortnightly, a London Midland Region practice at the time. On Call allowance and some overtime was included in this take-home amount, On Call being about 15 shillings per week.

It was an essential part of an SM's work each week to ensure that his staff received their pay on time and, of course, the correct amounts. The pay for the grade of all staff and any overtime, Sunday duty, etc, all came into this, as did such things as travelling time for relief signalmen. As we shall see later, at small stations in the 1950s and early 1960s the SM was involved in a good deal of work himself, including manual calculations in the days before computers or even calculators. Generally the pay work was undertaken by clerical staff and checked by the SM, and paybill auditors made spot checks.

Very often the SM took the pay out to signal boxes, level crossings, etc, as part of the weekly routine. At the same time the timesheets were collected, which the staff had filled in to show the hours they had worked during the week. Depending on the places to be visited, a number of

I do not know the story behind the blackboard message on the front of No 4663 – 'We want every Sunday' – but Sunday duties, including engineering work, brought in extra pay for many railway staff. The location is Bampton (Devon), on 1 May 1962.

arrangements could apply. In some places a taxi was routinely provided so that the SM could take quite large numbers of pay packets to another location in the area. This particularly applied where Engineers' platelayer staff were involved: you were paying wages even though it was another department's staff and the pay had been calculated by that department. At Elland I had a taxi one way, to Greetland, but had to walk back. Sometimes you could use your own car to deliver wages and receive a mileage allowance. At remote locations like Blea Moor, Goldthorpe and no doubt many other places, the SM would have the use of an engine and brake-van and would also deliver cans of water and paraffin to signal boxes and other locations.

The fact that the railway provided a secure occupation in times of unemployment, for example during the 1930s, and a regular wage, when other people were not so fortunate, was an obvious attraction. However, at other times this was not always the case. I can remember in 1966 BR lorry-drivers being granted an extra £1 per week in order to try and fill some of the vacant jobs.

In 1964 I once spent a day paying local staff who each had to produce a metal pay check before being handed a tin containing the cash. In the same year I was at a location where many guards were employed and the method for working out their pay was a 'daily appearance sheet', as it was known; these were batched up each day and sent to a regional centre. The problem was that the sheets for the last working day of the week might not get there in time, resulting in all the guards being one day short in their pay. It did not happen often, but some extra cash had to be found very quickly.

I recall an interesting item about payment of wages. In 1955, during the ASLEF strike, I was working 10 miles away from my home station, as a clerk. Travel was difficult but I was told not to worry about my pay as a Transfer Voucher was ideal for the situation. My home station wrote out one of these documents in duplicate, one copy being a debit, the other a credit. I was able to go to the booking office near the goods office where I was working, knowing that they had a credit to balance the cash that they handed over to me. The reverse was the case at the home station, the debit note balancing the reduced amount drawn from the bank. You didn't need to be a qualified accountant to work in a booking office, but you certainly learned the basics.

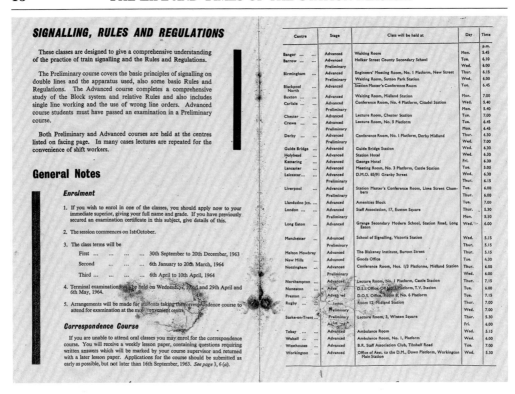

SIGNALLING, RULES AND REGULATIONS

These classes are designed to give a comprehensive understanding of the practice of train signalling and the Rules and Regulations.

The Preliminary course covers the basic principles of signalling on double lines and the apparatus used, also some basic Rules and Regulations. The Advanced course completes a comprehensive study of the Block system and relative Rules and also includes single line working and the use of wrong line orders. Advanced course students must have passed an examination in a Preliminary course.

Both Preliminary and Advanced courses are held at the centres listed on facing page. In many cases lectures are repeated for the convenience of shift workers.

General Notes

Enrolment

1. If you wish to enrol in one of the classes, you should apply now to your immediate superior, giving your full name and grade. If you have previously secured an examination certificate in this subject, give details of this.

2. The session commences on 1st October.

3. The class terms will be

First	...	...	30th September to 20th December, 1963
Second	...	...	6th January to 20th March, 1964
Third	...	...	6th April to 10th April, 1964

4. Terminal examinations will be held on Wednesdays, 22nd and 29th April and 6th May, 1964.

5. Arrangements will be made for students taking the correspondence course to attend for examination at the most convenient centre.

Correspondence Course

If you are unable to attend oral classes you may enrol for the correspondence course. You will receive a weekly lesson paper, containing questions requiring written answers which will be marked by your course supervisor and returned with a later lesson paper. Applications for the course should be submitted as early as possible, but not later than 16th September, 1963. See page 3, 6 (a).

Centre	Stage	Class will be held at	Day	Time
				p.m.
Bangor	Advanced	Waiting Room	Mon.	5.45
Barrow	Advanced	Holker Street County Secondary School	Tue.	6.10
	Preliminary		Wed.	6.00
Birmingham ...	Advanced	Engineers' Meeting Room, No. 1 Platform, New Street	Thur.	6.15
	Preliminary	Waiting Room, Sutton Park Station	Wed.	6.00
Blackpool North	Advanced	Station Master's Conference Room	Tue.	6.45
Buxton	Advanced	Waiting Room, Midland Station	Mon.	7.00
Carlisle	Advanced	Conference Room, No. 4 Platform, Citadel Station	Wed.	5.40
	Preliminary		Mon.	5.40
Chester	Advanced	Lecture Room, Chester Station	Tue.	7.00
Crewe	Advanced	Lecture Room, No. 5 Platform	Tue.	6.45
	Preliminary		Mon.	6.45
Derby	Advanced	Conference Room, No. 1 Platform, Derby Midland	Thur.	6.30
	Preliminary		Wed.	7.00
Guide Bridge ...	Advanced	Guide Bridge Station	Wed.	6.30
Holyhead ...	Advanced	Station Hotel	Wed.	6.30
Kettering ...	Advanced	George Hotel	Fri.	6.30
Lancaster ...	Advanced	Meeting Room, No. 3 Platform, Castle Station	Tue.	5.00
Leicester... ...	Advanced	D.M.O. 85/91 Granby Street	Wed.	6.30
	Preliminary		Thur.	6.15
Liverpool ...	Advanced	Station Master's Conference Room, Lime Street Chambers	Tue.	6.00
	Preliminary		Thur.	6.00
Llandudno Jcn....	Advanced	Amenities Block	Tue.	7.00
London	Advanced	Staff Association, 17, Euston Square	Thur.	5.30
	Preliminary		Mon.	5.30
Long Eaton ...	Advanced	Grange Secondary Modern School, Station Road, Long Eaton	Wed.	6.00
Manchester ...	Advanced	School of Signalling, Victoria Station	Wed.	5.15
	Preliminary		Thur.	5.15
Melton Mowbray	Advanced	The Blakeney Institute, Burton Street	Thur.	5.15
New Mills ...	Advanced	Goods Office	Tue.	6.30
Nottingham ...	Advanced	Conference Room, Nos. 1/3 Platforms, Midland Station	Thur.	6.00
	Preliminary		Wed.	6.00
Northampton ...	Advanced	Lecture Room, No. 1 Platform, Castle Station	Thur.	7.15
Nuneaton ...	Advanced	D.S.I. Office, Off No. 1 Platform, T.V. Station	Tue.	6.00
Preston ...	Advanced	D.O.S. Office, Room 8, No. 6 Platform	Tue.	7.15
Rugby	Advanced	Room 12, Midland Station	Thur.	7.00
	Preliminary		Wed.	7.00
Stoke-on-Trent ...	Preliminary	Lecture Room, 3, Winton Square	Thur.	5.30
	Advanced		Fri.	6.00
Tebay	Advanced	Ambulance Room	Wed.	5.15
Walsall	Advanced	Ambulance Room, No. 1, Platform	Wed.	6.00
Westhouses ...	Advanced	B.R. Staff Association Club, Tibshelf Road	Tue.	7.00
Workington ...	Advanced	Office of Asst. to the D.M., Down Platform, Workington Main Station	Wed.	5.30

Above 'Signalling, Rules and Regulations' courses listed in *Prospectus 1963-64: Further education for London Midland staff.* WA

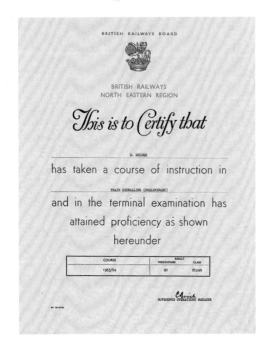

BRITISH RAILWAYS BOARD

BRITISH RAILWAYS
NORTH EASTERN REGION

This is to Certify that

D. HOLMES

has taken a course of instruction in

TRAIN SIGNALLING (PRELIMINARY)

and in the terminal examination has attained proficiency as shown hereunder

COURSE	RESULT		
	PERCENTAGE	CLASS	
1963/64	90	First	

MOVEMENTS OPERATIONS MANAGER

TRAINING

I don't remember specific training for potential SMs. Evening classes have already been mentioned, and the relevant subjects would be Passenger Station Work & Accounts, similarly Goods Station, as well as Railway Operating and Rules & Regs or part thereof (known as Train Signalling). I was fortunate to be a Management Trainee from September 1964 to July 1966, which came in the middle of my overall SM period of 1962-70. This training gave me a very good insight into vast numbers of jobs, including SM work at Hull Paragon and

Left The author passes his 'Train Signalling (Preliminary)' course in 1964. Evening classes were held in many subjects at District Office throughout the winter months.

Newcastle Central, signal boxes, loco sheds, marshalling yards and departments such as Engineering and Signal & Telegraph. You were more or less expected to study for the Institute of Transport exams during this period.

All staff could attend evening classes and study for the exams. A potential railway clerk would take an entrance exam, but possession of GCEs gave exemption when a new recruit joined BR.

In addition to the mandatory initial oral Rules & Regs exam and bi-annual renewal for the SM, other staff under his control would take exams in specific areas. Signalmen, guards and other staff were required to pass in Rules & Regs – this was all part of the ethos of keeping the railways safe for passengers and staff.

In the 1960s 'work study' became an important tool in the matter of reducing costs, particularly staff costs. Many SMs attended courses on this subject, and you might be sent home after the course with a remit to come up with some proposals for your area. I remember one senior SM being very annoyed, on the basis that any such measures would have been taken by him long ago. Some of these courses were so good that people from outside industry attended. At least one SM eventually left BR armed with Work Study qualifications, which was an indirect benefit to me as I then filled the resultant vacancy.

Generally BR did some very good work in training staff throughout the large number of jobs and departments involved. Some items of training were of a very practical nature. An SM needed to use the correct handsignals to drivers and guards to authorise movements in normal and emergency situations, as well as when you were doing some shunting yourself. If you were taking guards, fogmen, etc, through their exams you needed the practical training and experience to enable a proper job to be done. I also recall doing the necessary training to learn the correct use of air-brakes and fire extinguishers.

CONDITIONS OF EMPLOYMENT

This is not a subject to go into in great detail, but suffice to say that managers had a contract that covered hours of work, present salary, holiday arrangements, payment periods (eg four-weekly), sickness arrangements, pensions, notice to terminate employment, uniform and grievance procedures. These conditions were set out in accordance with the Contracts of Employment Act 1963.

DUTIES AND RESPONSIBILITIES

The 1950 Rule Book contained many instructions for the SM. Briefly they stated that all staff at a station, whether his own staff or not, were under his control and authority; all working must be strictly in accordance with the regulations; and all staff must have the necessary Rules & Regs, copies of working timetables and other notices as required for their particular duties.

The SM must have a thorough knowledge of the duties of his signalmen, make frequent visits to the signal boxes and sign the Train Register on each visit. He must carry out a daily inspection of the station and ensure that everything is clean and neat. He must make sure bye-laws and other notices are exhibited, report any complaints from the public, and ensure that Carriage and Wagon (C&W) examinations of rolling-stock are carried out and brake tests undertaken.

Overcrowded trains should have extra coaches added (this was known as 'strengthening' the train).

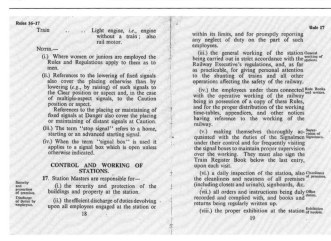

Part of Rule 17 in the BR 1950 Rule Book, providing instructions for Station Masters.

During fog and falling snow the SM had important duties regarding the provision, by the Engineer's Department, of fogsignalmen, each having the necessary detonators, flags, lamps, etc. He was to ensure that these men were at their posts, arranging call-outs if necessary out of hours, and arranging for handsignalmen if necessary in the case of signal failures. Platform staff were to call out the name of the station when a train arrived and the names of the stations where the train would call, as well as details of connecting services; Guards also had some of these duties.

Routine operating matters

An SM's duties varied from station to station, and the following will give an insight into some of the day-to-day operating – ie non-commercial work – involved. The SM was in a down-to-earth operating job and some of the duties may not seem to be what people might think of as SM's work. The station and area covered by the SM could include not just the station but also goods yards, junctions and sidings, and the latter might include both BR property and that of a private firm. He was responsible for all operating matters including observance of Rules & Regs everywhere within his patch.

Signal box visits: An SM visited signal boxes and manned level crossings on a routine basis to deliver pay and notices (of which more later). It was a convention that a signal box at the station would have a daily visit and others at least weekly, not including the pay visit. Out-of-hours visits – outside normal office hours of 9am to 5pm – were on a monthly basis. However, boxes could be open for one or two shifts, or the full 24 hours with three shifts – in some cases they were only open as required. This obviously affected the pattern of visits, which were in any case at irregular times, thus preserving the concept that the SM might appear at any time and on any day. He would sign the Train Register Book (TRB) on each occasion, including the time of his visit.

The following is a list of what the SM would check during the box visit. It is not a comprehensive list, as circumstances varied, including the design of the box, types of instruments and other items due to whichever pre-Grouping company was involved when the box was built and later modifications. It is, however, a fairly complete list of the main points, and often formed one of the main questions you had to answer at an interview.

• Check the box and signalling overall, including the performance of the

BRITISH RAILWAYS .... **Signal Box** **DOWN LINE** *Cont'd* *Fri – Jan 22 no' 1960* **11** BR. 24665

Description how Signalled	Circuits Received	REAR SECTION								ADVANCE SECTION						BLOCK BACK SIGNAL		Time Train is ready to Depart	REMARKS
		IS LINE CLEAR			Train Entering Section Received	Number of Engine	Train Arrived	Train Departed or Passed	Train Out of Section Signal Given	IS LINE CLEAR			Train Entering Section Given	Train Out of Section, Signal Given	Time Given or Received	Obstruction Removed Signal Given or Received			
		Received but NOT Accepted	Accepted under Regulation 5	Accepted under Regulation 3						Offered but NOT Accepted	Accepted under Regulation 5	Accepted under Regulation 3							
	H. M.	H. M.	H. M.	H. M.	H. M.		H. M.	H. M.	H. M.	H. M.	H. M.	H. M.	H. M.	H. M.	H. M.	H. M.		H. M.	
3			9 0	9 10	9 18				9 18	To (Down Shunt									3564
2122			30	33					46		950	950	10 0						3516. 63 Summa—
31			6x	AL	Man							930	935	950					
122			932	954					10 8		10 0	10 8	1021						7244 30 Scunthorpe
			No	Time	Signal	Received.	10-0 A.M.												
3			6x	Down	Shunt	Dep	10/15			1021	1021	1033							3564 13 Lutterworth
2122			1015	1020					10 30		1033	33	44						3578 65 KB
4			53	56	11 1				11 1		5611	3	1113						2524 10/41 WFG
122			11 9	115					114		1113	13	26						6670 52 Any Coly
122			1249	1255					1 5		1255	1 5	1 18						3522 50 Huck T
122			1 13	118					26		118	26	36						3534. 44. Leics
122			42	47					56		47	56	2 6						7246. 26 Scunthorpe
31			6x	Down	Shunt						2 6	211	23						
122			215	219					231		23	31	42						3538 60 KB
4			37	40	2 47				47		42	50	32						2552 3/29 WFG
2122			53	58					3 7		3 2	3 7	18						628 70 Newport
4			3 39	3 42	3 49				49		42	57	59						2014 3/31 WFG
					Potts		4.0 PM												
14			415	422					431		422	431	445						3530 52 Aleey
2122			31	31					41		45	45	54						18 S/L To Audal
122			46	53					5 0		545	5 0	512						3532. 50. Chy
122			522	528					36		528	538	49						3534 50 Newafool
					Pepper	off	5-30 PM												
31			48	53	6 1				6 1		53	6 3	6 14						
5			6 2	8 6					16		16	16	30						812 40 York
2122			16	16					29		30	30	41						6118 65 E Region
122			29	29					40		41	41	50						692 26 Staveley
4	37 M		43	50	6 57				57		50	57	7 10						36
122			57	59					7 6		710	710	17						814 12 Leic
31			76	78	215	717			15		17	17	29						
31	X	Dn	Sdp	8/7							8 15	8 15	8 31						
14			841	846					8 56		46	8 56	9 11						3862 58 Oct—
122			931	935					944		935	946	956						3538. 58 Oct—
4			1020	1023	1031				1031		1023	1036	56						2500
2122			31	36					48		50	50	11 2						8/265 Newport

Rugby Central Station Master J. E. Potts signs the Rugby Station signal box TRB when he visits at 4.00pm on Friday 22 January 1960.

signalman and box lad (where appropriate), especially that Rules & Regs were being followed.

- Check that stores and stationery are in order and up to date – this particularly applied to detonators on hand or in the detonator-placing machine being within date.

- Check the detonator machine and all other equipment, eg lever collars, track circuit indicators (where used), signal repeaters and signal lamp repeaters, and that seals are not broken (which they would have to be if points or point locks became locked by a track circuit failure).

- Check the block instruments to see that they reflect the current situation, and as shown in the Train Register Book (TRB).
- Check hand lamps (which should be lit if after dark), flags, coal, coke and paraffin.
- Check the signal and point levers, again according to the train situation when you entered the box and including any Signal & Telegraph disconnections, details of which should be in the TRB, which itself must be properly and neatly compiled and up to date.
- Everything must be clean and tidy.
- Deliver any notices or stores. There might, for instance, be 'delay' forms to deliver. This was not the most popular duty for the SM or signalman, as it meant that a train delay had taken place at the box maybe several days ago, and a guard had recorded it in his journal or Control had logged it at the time. The signalman involved would say that no signalman would delay a train without good reason, but the form

still had to be completed – nobody liked to be criticised in their professional duties even if it was unavoidable and no blame was attached.

TRBs were an important record of events, and even more so if there had been a mishap involving a later enquiry. In any case the TRB had to be properly compiled. A TRB check on a rota basis was necessary, and to do this the SM would withdraw the book for a particular day and arrange for the appropriate books from the adjacent boxes to be supplied, possibly by the SM at another station. A thorough check would then be made for every line of entry for the middle one of the three boxes against the relevant line at the next box, which should of course correspond to within a minute or so for each item. If a train was missing from the book at any of the boxes, this was a serious error and indicated an irregular event. The whole exercise was a simple but effective reflection of how signalmen were carrying out that part of their duties.

Trains passing through: At many main-line stations most of the trains would be passing through without calling at any of the SM's locations. The SM and his signalmen would thus be required to keep

At a station on a busy main line there would be a large proportion of trains passing through. Even though not calling at his station, the SM would be responsible for ensuring that traffic was kept moving, and that any problems such as train or signal failures would be dealt with quickly. No 6024 *King Edward I* rushes through West Drayton station with a down express at 11.49am on 6 July 1960.

traffic moving safely and without delays, even though there was no revenue directly involved.

Level crossings: There might be several of these or none at all depending on the topography. When making visits many of the routine items applied as described above for signal boxes. These included admin matters and pay, and checking any block or signalling equipment and the general safe working of the crossing.

Station work: From the earliest days an SM was required to see trains in and out at his station, keep trains running, maintain punctuality and explain any delays, together with signalmen's reports. In recent times there have been more and more unstaffed stations, and the days when nearly every station had its own SM are a distant memory. However, the SM still had a responsibility for punctual running at and tidiness of these stations.

From time to time District Office would require a census of passengers at the station or on trains. At the station this would simply consist of somebody standing around all day counting passengers joining or leaving trains. It was a job I undertook occasionally, including two full-day Summer Saturdays at Leeds Central in 1961. These census details were required to help decide future train services.

A pleasant event would be a visit by school children to the station. I always found that the expected problems did not occur, as the children had been well briefed beforehand not to run around and cause danger to themselves and others. Hopefully there were many future passenger journeys as a result, and there is still a lot of goodwill among the public towards the railways, possibly because of such visits and, of course, loco-spotting by large numbers of people over the years.

Detonators: There were strict instructions in the General Appendix about the conveyance, storage and examination of detonators, as well as the use of emergency detonator-placing machines at signals or at signal boxes. The SM had to check the condition of detonators and the date of manufacture shown on the detonator itself, assisted by a colour code: the detonator was painted overall in a colour for a particular year, and when they reached a certain age they were returned to Stores Department, even if they were still in good condition.

As well as signal boxes, drivers, guards and other departments also had detonators. Handsignalmen (flagmen) used them to protect obstructions and during engineering possessions of the line, while Guards similarly used them to protect a broken-down train, for example. Metal fastening strips were provided to attach a detonator to the rail or machine, and it had to be removed from the line as soon as the emergency or work was completed.

General operating items: Depending on the area and traffic dealt with, there might be various items of equipment for which an SM was responsible as regards their correct use.

A 'scotch block' was often a large piece of wood like a sleeper, that could be placed across the line in a siding to prevent movement of wagons. It was also an important aspect in the prevention of danger from vandals releasing wagon brakes, but the wagon might still be derailed at the scotch block. The blocks probably had a padlock or even wheels to make authorised use easier. A hand scotch might be used for the same purpose. Tow ropes or chains were specially authorised at some places where shunting would otherwise have been difficult due to the layout.

Above The different gradients of the two routes beyond the signal box at Killin Junction are noteworthy, and the points in the distance would be set for the siding to protect the 2.46pm service to Killin, about to depart to the left along the branch behind No 57276 on 18 June 1959. Killin Junction was a remote junction on the Caledonian Railway's Glasgow to Oban line. The station has now disappeared but Oban can still be reached via the North British route to Crianlarich, thence the original Caledonian line. As I recall, Killin Junction station was unusual in not having public road access.

Below Ledbury Tunnel is 1,323 yards long with a single line through the narrow bore, and a banking engine was provided to assist goods trains up the 1 in 70/80 gradient towards Worcester. There are many stories about steam trains slipping to a stand in the tunnel. No 6963, with the 11.50am Hereford-Paddington train, is emerging from the Worcester end on 28 June 1960, and a long sand drag is provided on the left to protect against runaways towards the tunnel.

Today's motorist will be familiar with a 'sand drag' at the foot of a steep hill, and a similar arrangement was used on the railway at some trap or catch points or similar locations where problems could be caused by a train overrunning a signal. Similarly a breakaway due to a coupling breaking on a steep gradient, or for that matter any other type of 'train divided' incident, could be mitigated by this apparently crude method. Air-braked trains have largely obviated the need for run-back catch points nowadays.

Long tunnels such as Standedge and Morley meant special instructions for the SM to observe if there was a mishap or, for example, a signal or block failure. Sometimes he was involved in a practical role. Over the years there have been many reports by drivers of 'bumps' experienced in tunnels, which of course involved examination of the line. It might turn out to be something, or it might not, but nothing is left to chance in the pursuit of railway safety.

The word 'annunciator' is still in use on the railways, and means an audible warning of the approach of a train; one such triggered by a track circuit, for instance, was used to warn staff if their view was obscured by trees, line curvature, etc.

Brake-vans were very important in the days before trains had continuous brakes, and most goods trains could not run unless they had one. The resultant cancellations were a constant problem until the arrival of the TOPS computer system and, eventually, the use of air-brakes, allowing most brake-vans to be dispensed with. Sometimes SMs had to arrange a brake-van census; this would be on a Sunday and would include all possible places where brake-vans might be located. Heating of brake-vans was always a problem, being fitted with only a crude stove – fuel had to be found for it, and loose fittings and rattling windows were often packed using newspapers. Another type of census was for BRUTES, those parcels trolleys seen at large stations.

Officers' special trains appeared from time to time, and might be from a department such as that of the engineer, where the SM would not be directly affected. If, however, it was your boss, the DOS, you had to be on your toes. The train might arrive at lunchtime, in which case it would stay for an hour or so. However, you would always know beforehand, as the Specials were shown in the weekly notices. In the 1960s increasing use was made of road transport, and therefore you might have no warning.

The SM would be in attendance at any places where an Inspection Special arrived, except perhaps if it was in use by the Engineer's Department. This photograph of No 43081 and an inspection saloon was taken at Peascliffe, near Grantham, on the afternoon of 24 October 1962. Note the express headlamps: the train would be signalled as 4 bells, 'Officers Special not requiring to stop in section'.

Contractors working near the line could be a problem. Safe walking routes for them and for BR staff had to be arranged and safe working practices enforced by the SM and, probably, other departments, especially the engineer's department.

In colliery areas the SM would not normally have any staff located at the pits, but there could be exceptions; for instance, a colliery at the end of a branch where Train Staff and Ticket working was in use required a BR man to be there.

The use of pilot or shunt engines is a large subject. These locos might be used as an area loco serving private sidings as well as shunting the local yard. They might also be used as banking engines on a regular basis, in addition to the shunting. The best-known jobs would be at larger stations, shunting parcels vans and moving empty passenger stock, but whatever the work the SM was always under pressure to reduce or curtail the use of such locos. Nowadays very few are to be seen at stations due to the types of trains in use and reductions in the traffics with which they were involved.

An SM was expected to know about and supervise the use of ground frames (GFs), of which there were several types and methods of operation. During remodelling of layouts and signalling, the installation of new GFs, perhaps where a signal box had previously been in use, meant that the SM had to learn and ensure the correct use of the equipment.

In carrying out his routine duties an SM would normally work either a half day or a whole day on Saturdays, and this would alternate according to whether you were On Call or not that weekend.

Derailments and diversions

We shall see more of these subjects under the heading of On Call. Obviously not all of these sort of incidents occurred out of hours, and for the present we shall have a look at the general arrangements for dealing with mishaps from the SM's point of view. As we shall see, many other people were also involved.

Derailments: On being advised of a derailment the SM would attend as quickly as possible. Some were clearly less of an emergency than others, such as a minor mishap in the sidings, but all had to be dealt with quickly. Injuries would be the first consideration, of course, although thankfully in the majority of cases there would be no injuries to passengers or staff. Many BR staff were trained in first aid; this has always been

This photograph was taken at Bidston at Saturday lunchtime on 3 November 1956, and illustrates the fact that to many people Saturday morning work was normal. A fair number of passengers are boarding the 12.45pm (SO) Seacombe-Wrexham Central local to return home to pleasant stations down the Wirral peninsula. SMs normally worked either Saturday mornings or all day.

encouraged and was very important if there was a delay in the arrival of an ambulance – access to some sites could be difficult.

The SM would then decide how to deal with the derailment. He would ring Control, which was not easy in the days before mobile phones or even access to GPO phones – signal phones were often the answer. It would be decided whether to re-rail using jacks, crane (often a steam crane) or ramps. The necessary departmental staff had to be called, again sometimes a phone problem, including Engineer's Department staff to assess the track and carry out subsequent repairs; Signal & Telegraph (S&T) staff to investigate any damage to signalling, point rodding, signal wires, interlocking, etc; and Carriage & Wagon (C&W) staff to assess damage to rolling-stock. Many staff did not have phones at home, although key people likely to be called to these incidents sometimes had them. Otherwise the SM might have to go to their houses.

The Shed Master's staff would also be called. If a loco was derailed, perhaps one pair of wheels, a visit by a van with ramps might be sufficient. In any case the toolvans, cranes, etc, came from the loco depots and were manned by their staff. Generally the whole re-railment job would be under the supervision of the Loco Department man, unless it was a very minor job not involving a loco. The SM would see to the operating side of things, such as line protection to ensure no other movements took place nearby during the re-railing process.

Control decided which depot would despatch the crane or toolvans. In a complicated area like the West Riding, each depot had its own area but would go elsewhere when necessary. Was just one line blocked or both? Was the main line affected at all? Would the toolvans or crane need to be remarshalled before going to a location at the end of a branch with no run-round facilities? These were the sorts of questions to be looked at by SM and Control. There is no doubt that

The ancient 'J69' station pilot, No 68599, has come off at the points at Lincoln on 8 September 1956, and the driver and shunter involved in the derailment confer at the end of the platform on the right. The SM will be involved in the re-railing arrangements and subsequent paperwork.

the work done by the toolvan staff was hard and difficult. After dark there might only be Tilley lamps as illumination when working under locos or wagons. The staff were usually taken off their normal work at the shed.

The SM would have to obtain sufficient details at an early stage to enable a report to be compiled. This meant deciding what had caused the accident. If it was due to track or points the Engineer's Department would often be unhappy, unless the cause was indisputable. For example, I once had a loco completely off the road in a siding, and when I pointed out that most of the keys were missing from the chairs securing the rails to the sleepers, it was clearly a case of 'road spread'. Points 'split' beneath a train might be the shunter's fault, or the engineer's. If the cause was difficult to

A GWR form authorising single-line working between Netherton and Windmill End in May 1913. It has been issued to the SM at Netherton by the Pilotman, Inspector Morgan.

determine it might be necessary for District Office to arrange a Joint Enquiry. This was a long, expensive business involving evidence from all departments concerned, but a conclusion had to be reached. Buffer-locking was a difficult problem in determining the cause of an accident, as the subsequent derailment might mean that the offending buffers were no longer locked. However, marks on the top of the rails leading up to a derailment could give a useful clue, which is what occurred at Royston (Yorks) in the early 1970s. If there was an incident at a colliery a Joint Report was produced and was signed by the SM and the National Coal Board (NCB).

The derailment might involve the SM in having to institute single-line working, and this was always an important point when taking your Rules & Regs exams. What were the principles and how would they be implemented at particular locations? This was a large subject involving, among other duties, the clamping of points and the use of detonators. A Pilotman would need to be appointed, perhaps a relief signalman or the SM himself, depending on the circumstances.

Diversions: Control would decide about the use of buses or taxis if diversions were required, and the SM was responsible for supervising passenger arrangements at his station involving road transport to other stations. It was not unknown for an SM to take people in his own car in the event of a mishap or even during planned Sunday work if there were problems.

The other side of the coin was if your line was the diversionary route. At a place like Knottingley the first you might know of a diversion was a 'Deltic' roaring past your window! It was such a normal route for planned Sunday diversions from, for example, Wakefield or York to Doncaster

No 60109 *Hermit* appears out of the gloom of a January Sunday afternoon in 1962 at Oakenshaw Junction with the 10.25am Sundays-only King's Cross-Leeds Central and Bradford Exchange train. It is on a diversionary route much used by trains unable to take their normal path due to engineering work. Local SMs would be involved in the planning and subsequent passenger arrangements.

via Knottingley and Askern, that a mishap or emergency engineering work meant a quick decision by Control during the week. The SM would be informed soon after the diversions commenced, and might then have the problem that one part of the route was only open on early and late turns. Would a night shift be necessary? If so, relief signalmen and crossing-keepers might be available, but possibly not if already fully occupied covering normal rest day, annual leave or sickness. In that case 12-hour shifts were probably the answer.

One Christmas the Wakefield to Doncaster diversionary route was required immediately due to a derailment elsewhere. The number of signal boxes and level crossings involved was a daunting prospect, as was the darkness of the early hours and about a foot of snow. However, my colleague and I had few problems – all the staff turned out without any complaints. They were true professionals, indeed. It was a case of knocking on a great many doors that freezing morning.

Derailments at collieries: These could often be dealt with by the NCB, as was the case when, in the early hours, a defective bottom door of a wagon meant that 10 tons or so of coal had to be shifted before the train could move. This coal was soon shifted by miners using crude struts as jacks and the most enormous shovels I have ever seen. It was not a coal board fault in this case, but sometimes the NCB would make a request for BR toolvans and men to be brought in for half a day or so to clear up one or two derailments of their own wagons with which they were unable to cope themselves.

Obstructions of the line: Many derailments did not affect main lines, but a main line could be blocked by prior arrangement for engineering work or in an emergency. These

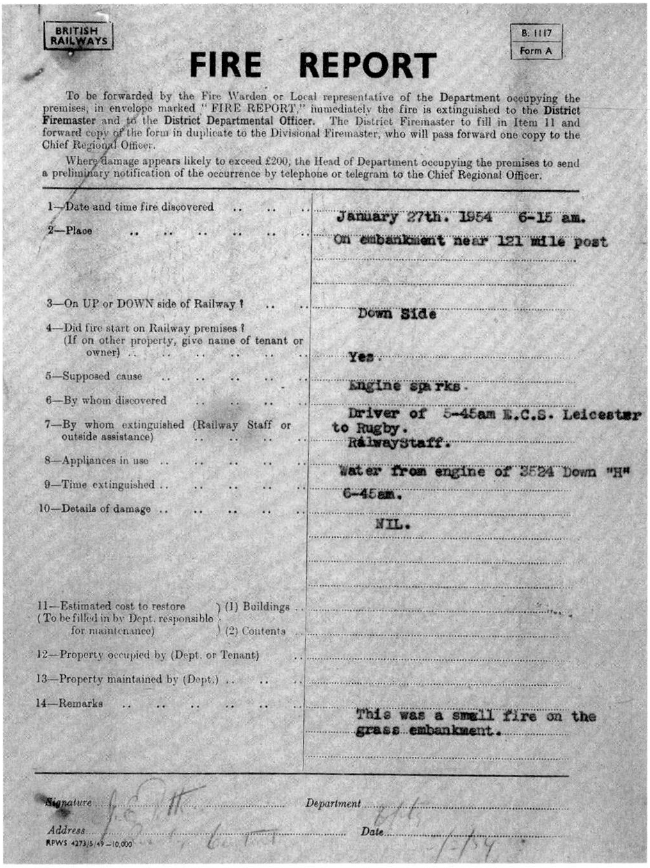

BRITISH RAILWAYS

B. 1117
Form A

FIRE REPORT

To be forwarded by the Fire Warden or Local representative of the Department occupying the premises, in envelope marked "FIRE REPORT," immediately the fire is extinguished to the **District Firemaster** and to the **District Departmental Officer.** The District Firemaster to fill in Item 11 and forward copy of the form in duplicate to the Divisional Firemaster, who will pass forward one copy to the Chief Regional Officer.

Where damage appears likely to exceed £200, the Head of Department occupying the premises to send a preliminary notification of the occurrence by telephone or telegram to the Chief Regional Officer.

1—Date and time fire discovered	January 27th. 1954 6-15 am.
2—Place	On embankment near 121 mile post
3—On UP or DOWN side of Railway ?	Down Side
4—Did fire start on Railway premises ? (If on other property, give name of tenant or owner)	Yes.
5—Supposed cause	Engine sparks.
6—By whom discovered	Driver of 5-45am E.C.S. Leicester to Rugby.
7—By whom extinguished (Railway Staff or outside assistance)	RailwayStaff.
8—Appliances in use	Water from engine of 3524 Down "H"
9—Time extinguished	6-45am.
10—Details of damage	NIL.
11—Estimated cost to restore (To be filled in by Dept. responsible for maintenance) (1) Buildings	
(2) Contents	
12—Property occupied by (Dept. or Tenant)	
13—Property maintained by (Dept.)	
14—Remarks	This was a small fire on the grass embankment.

Signature J. E. Potts Department Ops.
Address Rugby Central Date 27-1-54
RPWS 4273/5/49—10,000

Even a minor lineside fire between Rugby Central station and Shawell signal box caused by engine sparks involved the Rugby SM, Mr Potts, in a certain amount of paperwork. To accompany his report is an extract rewritten from the TRB in the Station signal box. *WA*

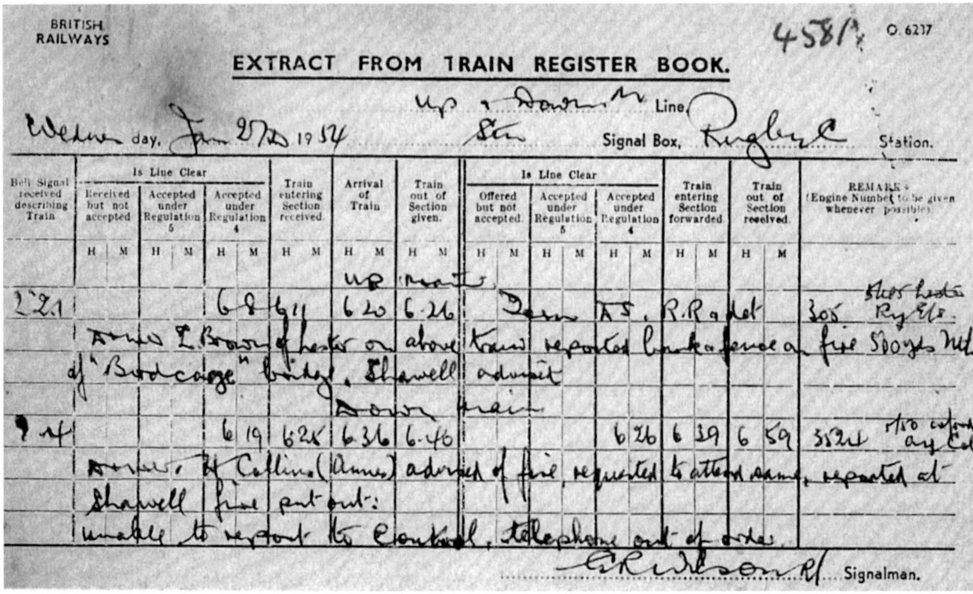

BRITISH RAILWAYS 4581 O. 6237

EXTRACT FROM TRAIN REGISTER BOOK.

Up & Down M Line.
Wednes day, Jan 27th 1954 Stn Signal Box, Rugby C Station.

Bell Signal received describing Train	Is Line Clear: Received but not accepted	Is Line Clear: Accepted under Regulation 5	Is Line Clear: Accepted under Regulation 4	Train entering Section received	Arrival of Train	Train out of Section given	Is Line Clear: Offered but not accepted	Is Line Clear: Accepted under Regulation 5	Is Line Clear: Accepted under Regulation 4	Train entering Section forwarded	Train out of Section received	REMARKS (Engine Number to be given whenever possible)
	H M	H M	H M	H M	H M	H M	H M	H M	H M	H M	H M	
				Up Main								
2-2-1			6 8	6 11	6 20	6 26	Down T.S. R.R. a/let					305 Stoke Leicester Rly Ets.
Driver E. Brown of Leicester on above train reported burning fence a fire 500 yds north of "Birdcage" bridge. Shawell advised												
				Down train								
1-4			6 19	6 25	6 36	6 46			6 26	6 39	6 59	3524 5.10 Woodford Col
Driver H. Collins (Annes) advised of fire, requested to attend same, reported at Shawell fire put out: unable to report to Control, telephone out of order.												

G. Richardson R/ Signalman.

emergencies could include, among others, any of the following:

- A derailment or loco failure
- A fire adjacent to the line
- The permanent way or a tunnel or bridge becoming unsafe
- A landslip, floods, or snowstorms
- A train becoming divided

The SM would ensure that any injuries were dealt with and that the Rules & Regs were complied with, and would advise Control the estimated time to clear the obstruction, whether toolvans were required, whether single-line working was needed, and any other action required.

Should the Engineer take possession of the line, were diversions necessary? If it was a serious blockage, should a higher-level enquiry be held to determine the cause and avoid a repetition?

Supervising clerical jobs

An SM supervised a great variety of office and outside staff. These varied according to the size of station and could affect the level of supervision; he might do the actual jobs himself, covering as required a job normally done by members of his staff or checking the work done by others. A good example of this is the booking office. If the SM had previously been a booking or goods office clerk it would be relatively easy for him to do any of the relevant tasks. He might be called in to help a ticket clerk strike a balance. He would be familiar with the office work, with the Edmondson card ticket racks and the pillar date-stampers with metal numbers to be changed at the end of each day ready for next morning. He would check booking office and parcels office books and sign the month-end returns, as well as observing that correct procedures were being followed. From the early days of the railways the maintenance of complete

and up-to-date records was a specified duty for an SM.

The goods element would generally be smaller, as a Goods Agent was in charge of medium-sized or larger depots. The accommodation in the parcels and goods offices would often consist of sloping desks, high stools, coal fires and gas lamps, while the office windows might have bars.

Admin matters

The number of staff supervised by the SM affected how much he was involved in day-to-day admin, from doing most of it himself at small stations to having chief clerks at large stations. The ordering of stores and stationery was a routine matter.

Fuel: In the days of coal or coke fires the SM had to ensure that all points had enough fuel. The signalman on nights or anybody else working during periods of very cold weather rightly expected to have enough fuel to keep warm. The SM ordered a wagon of coal, which came directly from a colliery even though it was ordered via the stores system. He had to make sure it was ordered in good time and make arrangements for placing it in the appropriate siding. Who was going to unload it? As a booking clerk covering the porter's job, this occasionally fell to me. There are many stories of coal being picked up from the lineside if staff were running short, or a loco fireman supplying a few choice lumps to a signal box. During a coal strike and even for some weeks afterwards it helped if you had a secret supply hidden away, which was something I had at one station.

Booking offices, waiting rooms, staff rooms and goods offices all needed supplies of fuel. Sometimes an SM would deliver emergency supplies to signal boxes. On the North Eastern Railway it was common practice for the SM to run the coal sales business at his station, a useful addition to his wages. This was, of course, later superseded by coal merchants running the businesses, as in other parts of the country.

Uniforms: The SM and a large number of his staff were entitled to uniform clothing, although clerical staff were normally an exception. It was a tradition from the early days of the railways for staff to have the appropriate uniform of their company, and this continues today: it identified you as a member of staff and could be very smart and designed to impress customers with the status of the company as well as your job within it. Obviously there were other reasons, including the need to deal with dirty jobs such as shunting or handling parcels.

Many jobs involved working in all weathers. The railway overcoat, or those black mackintoshes with a distinctly rubbery smell, were well known; the latter was my only piece of uniform during my first few months as an SM. Handed to me by a friend who had given up being an RSM, it gave me an identity before the full uniform and hat arrived.

There were ordering procedures for obtaining clothing from the Stores Department. Measurements were sent in and, as well as delays from time to time,

there were inevitable misfits and items having to be returned. The SM's double-breasted jacket was hardly fashionable in the 1960s, and the heavy hat, with the designation 'Station Master' woven in gold and a badge with a background indicating the Region, was not easy to wear.

Health and Safety: This was known under other names but was certainly part of the job, and included the safety of both passengers and staff. There were accident reports to compile and the need to ensure that 'Prevention is better than Cure'. This was the title of a marvellous book produced by the London, Midland & Scottish Railway (LMS) in 1924, with a large number of carefully staged photos out on the line as well as at stations and yards.

Security of premises was another important duty. This was made easier at larger stations if Railway Police were located there to deal with crime prevention and so many other aspects that are still as relevant today as they ever were.

Railwaymen's Year Book (1950 edition): I have a copy of this book and still refer to it sometimes. It gave useful

Rugby Central won a prize for cleanliness and tidiness in 1960, and the station staff (with SM Ernie Potts second from left) pose for a photograph to mark the event. *V. W. Long, Will Adams collection*

information for all railway staff in the early days of BR. There were Staff Suggestion Schemes, First Aid classes and competitions, welfare arrangements, a Staff Savings Bank, and residential training on each Region, as well as evening classes. Although not relevant, it is delightful to read that BR main-line coaches are painted 'Crimson Lake with Cream panels', rather different from some descriptions given for this colour scheme. There is mention of Best Kept Station awards and that bullhead rails weigh 95 pounds per yard and flat bottom 109 pounds, this latter now being the standard type. Wooden sleepers measured 9ft x 10in x 5in.

SM's offices and meetings: An SM usually had his own office, but this was often not the case at smaller stations. He also had SMs' meetings to attend, which were on a District, later Divisional, basis. You did not wear uniform at these events, which were usually held in a hotel near District Office. This was all very well unless you were in lodgings with a limited wardrobe available. This happened to me at one meeting in Derby in 1962 – I was the only person wearing uniform. Sometimes the meeting would be preceded by a discreet staff representative session where a volunteer SM would take your views and speak on your behalf to Management about any concerns that the gathered SMs might have. Generally the meeting gave you the chance to speak to District Officers and hear what was going on from a wider angle than your sometimes parochial perspective.

SM Discussion Group meetings might be held in the evening. These were purely voluntary, with no connection to the routine SMs' meetings. However, if you were fortunate to have someone like Bishop Eric Treacy coming to give a talk and show his slides of the Lake District, it was an occasion not to be missed. After 40 years it is a memory that I treasure.

Civic duties: BR staff were encouraged to take part in civic duties such as being on the Town Council, possibly even becoming Mayor or perhaps a local Magistrate. It was a feather in the cap for the railways to employ people engaged in such important duties. Generally time off would be arranged, or sometimes a permanent early turn so that afternoon meetings could be attended. For four years while an SM I was a member of a local tribunal as an employer's representative, which brings to mind an amusing incident. There was a local election in the town and one party stuck a poster on the low parapet of a railway bridge over a busy footpath. The other party came to see me, furious at being outwitted by their opponents. In any case they hadn't been able to remove the poster as it was so well stuck and it was my bridge anyway. The solution was obvious – place their poster next to it. Later I used the same location for excursion posters.

Getting jobs covered: The SM would have staff problems, often due to the 24-hour, seven-days-a-week nature of the work. Many call-outs would be due to staff reporting sick for a 6am start or even, occasionally, going off sick in mid-shift. Generally the DSI at District Office would deal with signalmen's cover, but you might still have to go and fetch the man required to take up duty. Crossing-keepers were a local responsibility, and if there were many crossings it could be quite difficult. Twelve-hour working was often necessary for many types of staff if there was a lack of relief – some people were happy to work 12-hour shifts because of the overtime, but some were not, such as unmarried staff who didn't need the extra money. Many people were keen on overtime, working rest days or Sundays, while sometimes jobs remained vacant due to planned closures.

SMs would often use their own cars in the days when car ownership became more usual and staff had to be fetched. At one time telegrams would be used – GPO telegrams were free of charge to BR for many years. If a vehicle was provided, such as a 5cwt van, a BR domestic licence was issued after a suitable test had been passed. This was in addition to the normal public driving licence.

VIPs: Finally in this section I would mention the pleasant duty that an SM might have, that of meeting VIPs, although obviously this was more likely to occur at larger stations.

Weekend working arrangements

The SM's visit to signal boxes and other locations on pay day usually included delivery of weekly and weekend notices. A further visit on Saturday morning, if required, would be partly to deliver any last-minute notices. Generally notices would include Special Traffic Notices (STNs) and advices showing excursions,

relief trains, etc, together with any other publications, such as amendments to manuals. However, the main reason for the Saturday visit would be weekend working arrangements. The signalmen would have had time to read the notices delivered on pay day and any changes to box opening times because of engineering work would by then have been arranged. Usually the DSI, centrally located at District level and in charge of relief signalmen's rosters, would have been involved. Often a District Inspector was allocated to specific jobs such as line possessions out in the District at the weekend.

The notices consisted of, among other things, the weekly Permanent Way (PW) book showing midweek and weekend engineering work, temporary speed restrictions and many other items needed by signalmen to do their jobs. Engineer's staff, S&T, traincrews and others also had this book as an essential part of their work. Then, as now, a great deal of engineering work had to be done at the weekend, and line possessions, train diversions, box openings and bus substitutions all had to be checked by the

Well-used copies of a 1966 Special Traffic Notice and an 'ME2' notice informing staff of temporary speed restrictions etc, such as would have been distributed by the SM to all interested parties.

SM in time for the pay day and Saturday visits to ensure that all relevant items in the various notices had been covered and delivered in time. In an area with level crossings it would mean many more visits so that everyone involved had full details. Single-line working (SLW) might be planned for the weekend or perhaps on a routine basis during the week. I once spent time each day for a couple of weeks putting in SLW for a routine bridge repair job. I was then free to carry out my normal duties as I was not the Pilotman. On occasions, however, I would be arranger as well as Pilotman at the weekend.

SOCIAL ACTIVITIES

It was always a pleasant and worthwhile part of life at a station to have social activities, usually in the evenings or at weekends. Obviously shift working and the size of the station and the number of people employed had a bearing on how many could attend. Office trips were very popular at one time, and railway social clubs, for example the BRSA, and places like Swindon Works would sometimes go to great lengths to arrange for staff and families to have a day out together. Of the office trips that I attended, none were from stations; one was from a goods depot in Leeds to visit Whitby, when the through route via Pickering was still available, and the second was a Divisional Office trip to Seahouses. These trips took place during the normal week, with people covering each other's jobs for the day.

Retirements and presentations of long-service awards always provided enjoyable opportunities for a social evening in a pub. Sometimes they were just at the station during the day, and probably more of your colleagues would be there in that case. Social clubs might include running a cricket team and children's Christmas parties with visits to a pantomime. Jumble sales were always an essential fund-raising event, and great fun.

First aid, or the Ambulance Movement as it was once known, was, to an extent, part of the job, but did have social elements too. In the 19th century some SMs arranged St John Ambulance classes as well as organising concerts in aid of railway charities. I set up and attended first aid classes in the late 1960s and took part in one first aid competition.

Overall the social, sporting and first aid side of railway life reinforced my view that we were part of a great railway family throughout the country, and it is pleasant to know that many of these activities continue today.

First-aiders wearing St John Ambulance badges on their caps and carrying a stretcher, pose for the photographer at Shipley Junction. *John Ryan Collection*

Above It is not possible to read any of the inscription on the shield, but the Waverton SM and his staff are clearly proud of their achievement, whatever it was! *John Ryan collection*

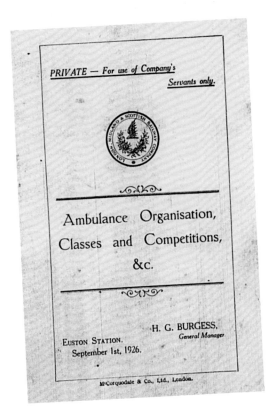

PRIVATE — *For use of Company's*
Servants only.

Ambulance Organisation,
Classes and Competitions,
&c.

H. G. BURGESS,
General Manager

EUSTON STATION.
September 1st, 1926.

McCorquodale & Co., Ltd., London.

Left An LMS booklet of 1926. *WA*

ON CALL AND CALL-OUTS

This is another large subject and I shall endeavour to select some of the more interesting aspects as well as explaining the On Call arrangements. Most SMs had On Call commitments and often alternated with an adjacent SM. At East Leake I was On Call alternate weeks, covering Ruddington as well. The Ruddington SM similarly covered my area alternately. Effectively this involved coverage, out of normal office hours, of the GCR main line from the bridge over the Trent southwards to the Loughborough up Distant signal.

You had a half day off on Wednesday afternoon then commenced being On Call at 0001hrs on Thursday morning. Saturday was a full day at work, and On Call finished at midnight on Wednesday. When Off Call you had a half day off duty on Saturday afternoon.

Usually the call-out would originate with a telephone call from Control, or perhaps a member of the station staff knocking on your door. If there was a long job, for example a re-railing operation going on all day, it would be normal for the SM dealing with it to hand over to the On Call man at about teatime unless, of course, he himself was On Call. Many calls were due to staff not turning up for duty at 6am; sometimes this or other admin matters could be dealt with over the phone, and was known as a telephone call-out. One SM of the old school whom I knew still liked to visit the cinema each week, even when On Call. This was easily arranged: Control would be given the phone number of the cinema and, if there was a call-out, a suitable message was transmitted onto the cinema screen by the projectionist.

The lack of phones at home or, of course, today's ubiquitous mobile was a problem, particularly as mentioned earlier in the derailments section. Signal phones might be useful up to a point if you were ringing the signalman, but how could he or anyone else contact you if necessary? What if there was a second emergency affecting you? This was the case at Sharlston one winter's afternoon as a pea-souper of a fog came down at nightfall. With a Class 40 diesel-electric loco 'off all wheels' blocking one line and the sudden requirement to run diverted trains over the other due to a mishap elsewhere, it was a difficult situation to say the least. My colleague had been called away to assist drivers at another location as the fog was so bad. In addition, the toolvan staff were still re-railing the Class 40. A handsignalman was sent to tell me about the diversions and I made appropriate arrangements. Even so, the first Class 47-hauled train doing about 60mph in nil visibility was quite a shock.

Turning now to more mundane matters, there follow brief details of some call-outs at Castleford in the late 1960s. Some happened several times and were over quite a long period of time.

Level crossings: car hit Cutsyke gates; bolts up on crossing and gateman needed to pull gates across due to signalman having problems; windman needed for gates due to gale force winds; gate failure. **Mechanical problems:** points failure; points run through; defective signal; light out on temporary speed restriction sign; block failure; calling out S&T lineman for various other problems including telephone failure, block bell failure, and track circuit failure; broken fishplate; possible buckled rail due to hot weather. **Staff matters** (including calling out staff for some of the above incidents): fetching fogsignalmen, guard (not my staff but living in the area), signalmen, platelayers, handsignalmen and relief signalmen. **Derailments** (particularly at collieries): the track tended to be poor in the days before 'merry-go-round' (MGR) bunkers were built and the new track associated with them, after which most of the NCB sidings were no longer required. (Unfortunately this contributed to the demise of NCB steam locos, still in use several years after BR steam ended in 1968. NCB steam locos were even used to haul MGR sets under the bunker at Glasshoughton, while BR steam locos worked some MGR sets on the main line in the North East at one time.) **Weather:** wires down on the Kippax branch due to heavy snowfall and consequent block and phone failure – Pilotman working necessary on what was, in any case, a single-line branch. **Crime:** break-ins at Cutsyke and Castleford Central stations; also at Lofthouse Junction, a remote signal box and an easy target for thieves; brasses stolen from wagon axleboxes; telegraph

At Morpeth on 30 December 1965 some new air-braked 'merry-go-round' trains have been pressed into service. In this case the train, headed by No 65842, has reversed at Morpeth and is heading in the direction of Blyth on a pre-MGR working.

wires stolen on several Saturday evenings causing block failures (despite the SM and police attending, the thieves made off each time empty-handed in the darkness).
Animals: Deliver urgent livestock, eg day-old chicks; remove heavy, injured dog from line with assistance from RSPCA.
Public: opening the station on Sunday afternoon for someone to collect urgent lost luggage.
Signalling: opening and working Castleford Old Station signal box after the early turn man phoned in sick. The DSI arranged a relief man, but the box had to be opened in the meantime. I annoyed a driver of a diesel multiple unit (DMU) by not pulling off the Distant signal, then the phone rang and it was the fireman of the first train that I had dispatched up the branch to Allerton Bywater Colliery – they were now returning and why were they being held up at the Home signal?

At East Leake in December 1962 I was asked to call out the fogmen for Ruddington. This was at the time when the so-called smog (a combination of smoke and fog that produced really appalling conditions before clean air regulations helped reduce pollution) was, thankfully, nearly coming to an end. Having driven through the smog for several miles to get to Ruddington box, I found on arrival that the weather was starting to clear and the fog marking point could now be seen (this point was usually a designated signal or a distance of at least 200 yards, as specified in the Signalmen's General Instructions). The fogmen were, therefore, not required.

In the Cudworth area, among many call-outs, was one to Monk Bretton, where a heavy sand train had to be divided as the loco was unable to haul it up the steep incline; unfortunately the rear portion ran away and was derailed at the catch points protecting the main line.

At Darfield a member of the public reported a railway bridge as being in a dangerous condition. I met the Bridge Inspector of the Engineer's Department and a local policeman who conducted us to the bridge. It turned out to be a pedestrian tunnel under the Midland main line, which was on a high embankment; the roof of the tunnel was supported by numerous heavy wooden props and one was out of place. The Bridge Inspector said he would get it fixed. Then as now these inspectors were also kept busy with numerous 'bridge bashes', usually by lorries.

One very strange call-out was at Barnsley. It was late on a Saturday evening and a reveller had driven his car through a fence and dropped down into a cutting, fortunately without serious injury. I arrived together with an Engineer's Department man and it was obvious, even in the darkness, that there was no railway track in the cutting. It was, in fact, an old Hull & Barnsley Railway line lifted years previously. The Engineer chap made a temporary job of mending the fence and promised to arrange a proper job at first light.

At Cudworth a tamping machine was derailed on the goods line and an axle was broken. It was a 'chicken and egg' situation: had the axle broken and caused the derailment, or had the machine derailed first, causing the axle to break? On another occasion at Cudworth vandals threw a metal ladder on to the line. I flagged down an approaching Class 37 on a coal train and asked the driver to draw forward so that I could get the ladder onto the brake-van.

One early morning at Oakenshaw snow had fallen and a Healey Mills to Tinsley freight had been standing at a signal for an hour. It was suspected that the signal was being held at danger, even though cleared by the signalman, due to snow in the trailing points just ahead of the train. I checked the points and they were fitting, so the train was authorised to proceed and the ganger attended not long afterwards to check all the points for snow problems.

Finally, three more unusual occurrences. One summer Saturday afternoon a holiday train arrived at York and two teenage girl students complained that hooligans had thrown their rucksack out of the window. The train had been delayed at a signal at Ferrybridge at the time, which was confirmed by the guard. A further clue was that the girls had been travelling in a particular coach on the train. Armed with this information it was possible to locate, within 30 yards or so, where the rucksack might be. Despite a lot of undergrowth and brambles I was able to find it and hand it to the guard of the next York train.

Streethouse level crossing was a former signal box now equipped with lifting barriers. Due to gale-force winds one barrier, when vertical and with the crossing open to busy road traffic, was being blown down sufficiently to set off the red flashing lights and ringing bells, thus stopping the traffic.

At Askern there was an agreement that the resident shunter would prepare each outgoing loaded MGR train by coupling and shortening the 'instanter' couplings, connecting the air-brake pipes and dealing with the valves. This had to be done 14 times for a full set of wagons and the guard's booked time was thus reduced with, of course, a brake test still needed. The call-out arose because the shunter was off sick and no relief was available. It was hard work if you were not used to it.

TRAFFICS DEALT WITH

It is easy to forget just how many types of traffic were dealt with in the 1960s. An SM usually had a mixture of passenger, goods and parcels traffic, the latter usually being sent by passenger train or in dedicated parcels trains. My particular experiences had a bias towards freight, but we will look at all three types of traffic.

Above Mail and parcels traffic by rail was once extensive. The up 'Northumbrian' calls at Durham on 27 September 1961, and large numbers of mail bags are being loaded onto barrows. The driver of the bank engine, No 67689, is awaiting the tip to start assisting the heavy express train up the gradient to the south in a busy scene typical of a medium-sized main-line station.

Below At the terminus of the short branch line from Coaley Junction to Dursley it was convenient for a GPO mail van to be on the platform for the loading and unloading of mail bound to and from main-line trains at the junction. Note the 10-ton 'Vanfit' marshalled next to 0-6-0PT No 1630 in this 28 June 1960 picture.

Above At Thurso, the most northerly station on BR, ex-Caledonian 4-4-0 No 54482 awaits departure with the 3.35pm service to Inverness on 3 May 1961. A BR lorry is alongside the train and large numbers of parcels are being loaded. The overall roof and goods yard complete the picture.

Below This label is for livestock carried by passenger-rated train, and includes details of feeding and watering arrangements.

Parcels

These would be conveyed to or from the station by the customer or might be C&D, ie collected and/or delivered by the railway. In this case a larger station would usually be involved. At East Leake a van came out from Nottingham Victoria on alternate days for this purpose, serving villages like Thrumpton and Barton-in-Fabis. PLA (Passengers Luggage in Advance) was very popular: large numbers of people took their holidays in Britain and travelled by train, and they could send their luggage in advance of their journey; if collected and delivered it cost 5s 6d, or 2s 9d if it was only collected or delivered. It could be insured against damage for a small fee. University luggage was also considerable at certain times of the year. Some traffics were so large that

BRITISH RAILWAYS (_____ Region) USE BLOCK LETTERS _____ B.R. 21657 _____ 19____

Loaded Time _____ 19____

LIVESTOCK
PASSENGER RATED TRAFFIC

FROM _____

TO _____

_____ Region _____ Secn.

VIA _____

Sender _____

No. and Description of Animals _____

Watered and/or Fed at _____ Time _____ Date _____ Time _____ Date _____

| Required to be Milked not later than | CARRIAGE CHARGES |
| Paid £ s. d. |

Time _____ Date _____ | To Pay £ s. d. |

Consignee _____

Address _____

Vehicle No. _____

LABEL TO BE RETAINED BY RECEIVING STATION

Milk is a traffic that has completely disappeared from the railway. On the right of this view of Torrington on 30 June 1960 the lorry driver is leaning out of his cab as he reverses towards the churns on the down platform. Note also the loading gauge and warehouse in the goods yard, and the heater for the water crane. No 41313 is at the head of a portion of the 'Atlantic Coast Express' for the early part of its journey to Waterloo.

complete trains would be provided in addition to smaller items by passenger train: these included mail (letter or parcel post), newspapers, fish (including empty boxes going back to the ports), pigeons and milk. Some early DMUs did not have enough space for the considerable parcels traffic of the time, so steam-worked parcels trains could be seen. Many types of livestock were sent by rail, including day-old chicks; even this traffic needed full train loads from the main firms. Market traffic including tomatoes and sprouts often went by goods train. Circus trains, cattle trains – the list is long but the SM had his part to play in many of them.

An SM might well have to collect outstanding goods accounts from customers and unpaid passenger fares where a passenger had been allowed to travel on a promise-to-pay-later-basis – not an easy job.

Excursion traffic

This was extensive, and not just in the summer. In the industrial North the excursion season started with Easter when trains, stored all winter, some of them composed of non-corridor stock, would be brought out of the sidings. The Rugby League Cup Final at Wembley soon followed and could easily produce a dozen trains. At East Leake on 12 May 1962 eight Wembley-bound trains passed through within 3 hours, all except one being hauled by 'Jubilee' Class steam locos. As SM at Castleford I would have been failing in my duty had I not travelled on one of the six trains in 1969 when the local team won through to the Final; and this was repeated a year later. There were, of course, also excursions for many other sporting events, including football and racing in particular; some racecourses had and still have their own stations.

In the background, beyond No 69837 at Hull Paragon on 28 April 1956, are quite a lot of football supporters making their way to the train for Boothferry Park. Several trains ran from Paragon and direct football specials from further afield could also serve Boothferry Park, where there was direct access from the single 200-yard platform to the turnstiles of the Hull City ground.

A Summer Saturday return holiday train, the 1.28pm (SO) Cleethorpes to Nottingham Victoria behind No 61870, is being met at Edwinstowe on 26 August 1961 by a porter in the uniform of the early 1960s. Note the attractive lamp cases and station buildings. The two cans on the far platform appear to be water containers.

Above A Summer Saturday train, the 7.58am (SO) from Derby, passes Newlay & Horsforth station behind 'Jubilee' No 45692 heading for Glasgow St Enoch on 16 July 1960. There are extensive station gardens, gas lamps and stabled coaching stock to be seen. The signal box is in the distance and there are some young locospotters on the left.

Below Two 'B1s', Nos 61387 and 61295, are storming up the gradient at Laisterdyke with stock for an Easter Monday excursion from Drighlington to Scarborough on 3 April 1961; Scarborough is one of the traditional excursion destinations from the West Riding. Note the train number chalked on the smokebox door and the board on the buffer-beam.

Above The excursion train number can also be seen on the buffer beam of 'Jubilee' No 45739 *Ulster* at York on 30 May 1966. At one time it would have been very unusual to see any LMS-type locos working to Scarborough, but by 1966 things had changed. The fine station roof is seen to good advantage.

Below Veteran 'Terrier' 0-6-0T No 32646 stands at Havant with the 2.35pm (Sundays-only) Havant-Hayling Island train on 2 June 1957. An amazing number of people travelled down the branch on this fine Sunday afternoon; I recorded three of these 'Terriers' providing a regular shuttle service, connecting with the main-line trains.

On the East Coast Main Line on this Summer Saturday, 20 August 1960, there was a constant procession of steam-hauled long-distance trains, many conveying holidaymakers. 'A2' No 60504 passes Tuxford with the 11.40am (SO) King's Cross-Newcastle train. Note the large group of exchange sidings in the background, but little traffic on hand. The track layout on the right is very complex, with a lot of points to be worked by Tuxford Junction signal box.

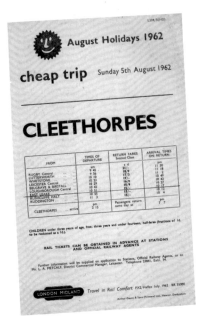

'Garex' (Guaranteed excursion) trains, usually hired by social clubs, would mean the SM being on duty on a Sunday morning in the summer – these trains usually worked on Sundays as the stock would be needed on Saturdays and Bank Holidays for normal holiday travel. There were also many other types of excursion, such as day, half day and 'mystery' trips.

Air displays and holiday relief trains brought in large numbers of passengers. At busy weekends it was common in the North, particularly for Wakes Weeks, to have, for example, a Bradford Exchange to King's Cross train starting back at somewhere like Hebden Bridge. This helped to achieve the objective of providing as many stations and passengers as possible with services to an extended range of holiday destinations when the mills closed for the week.

Inevitably there were excursion returns to be filled in advising District Office how many people had travelled and the receipts. This, together with routine census arrangements, helped in planning next year's trains. The trains would carry numbers, sometimes chalked, on the smokebox, and the details would be in the STN to assist signalmen, station staff and others when dealing with the trains.

SMALL STATIONS

At smaller stations, particularly the traditional country or branch-line locations, the SM did a lot more of the day-to-day down-to-earth jobs. At one time he would also work the signal box on a regular basis.

General duties
The SM would book tickets, deal with parcels, including delivering urgent items, and see the trains in and out as well as possibly covering the porter's or clerk's jobs if necessary. In the office the pay

would be worked out manually including income tax and sticking NHI stamps onto documents. The cash might have to be collected from the bank and the booking and goods office receipts paid in. At some small stations the wages cash would arrive in a leather pouch sealed with wax and the imprint of the sending station. In the reverse direction the receipts would also be sent in a sealed pouch. (After all these years the aroma of melting wax and, even more so, the burning in of new gas mantles remain in the memory!) The pay would be put into packets for collection by Permanent Way (PW) staff and station staff, or for delivery to other locations.

Shunting
The SM might have regular shunting duties at small stations, or perhaps he would just cover for a shunter or porter who was unavailable. Generally you would be working with the guard in this case. On occasion a signalman, keen to earn some overtime, would volunteer to do the shunter's job. A shunt pole was 6 feet long by 2 inches in diameter, made of ash wood or sometimes of metal.

Small goods yards
Very often there was a small goods yard and the SM had various outdoor duties to consider. Wagon sheets, sometimes known as tarpaulins, were 16 feet square and needed to be fastened over a wagon when in use or otherwise folded in accordance with the instructions in the Working Manual. There could be grain sacks for hire to farmers, or handled in loaded or empty condition. This would generally but not always be in agricultural areas. Even a place like Elland was involved in an indirect way as there were grain merchants in the area and the progress of loaded sacks and the subsequent handing back empty had to be monitored – sack auditors checked on the

Above 4-4-0 No 54495 is doing a little light shunting at Helmsdale on the morning of 3 May 1961, the kind of activity in which the local SM might be involved. On this bright spring morning the fine-looking Caledonian engine is in very clean external condition.

Below left A Lancashire & Yorkshire Railway shunter poses with his shunt pole just after the First World War. *John Ryan collection*

Below right Forteviot, between Perth and Stirling, possessed a typical small goods yard with crane, warehouse, loading dock and a couple of wagons. The up Postal, behind 'V2' No 60919, is passing at considerable speed.

situation. Wagon ropes as well as sheets might be in use.

At one time, in agricultural localities, extra staff were needed at certain times of the year to deal with sugar beet, rhubarb, peas and many other seasonal traffics. Coal was, of course, a very important item, and many small goods depots kept going on this basis. It could be domestic or industrial, or maybe coal spillages (ie salvaged coal from marshalling yards) would be dealt with in a few places. There might be a cattle dock and, usually, a small warehouse, and these were often retained when the goods yard closed to be rented out (as were many station buildings after closure).

Finally, mention should be made of returned empties, large quantities of which were often handled at small passenger or goods stations. The crates or

Right Grain sack hire charges, 1951.

Below A hand-operated crane in a typical small goods yard. *John Ryan collection*

BRITISH RAILWAYS

The Railway Executive (Eastern, London Midland, North Eastern and Scottish Regions) hereby give notice of the following revised Charges on which their Grain Sacks are let out on hire, **to take effect on and from 1st March, 1951 :—**

(a) **Sacks hired empty.**
   1¾d. per sack for a period not exceeding 7 days, including dates of hire and return.

(b) **Sacks forwarded full by Railway Executive Transport.**
   A further 14 days allowed from the date of despatch if forwarded full by Railway Executive Transport.

(c) **Sacks detained beyond the above periods—Demurrage Charges.**
   1d. per sack per week, or part thereof, will be charged after the above periods.

(d) **Sacks hired (full) by Consignee or Transferee under fresh Contract.**
   The charge for demurrage, as in (c), will commence when the period specified in (b) under the previous contract has expired.

   Note. Sunday, Good Friday, and Christmas Day (England and Wales) or New Year's Day (Scotland), will be treated as normal days.

(e) **Stay Hire.**
   A charge to stay hire of 10s. 0d. per sack in addition to other charges which may be due, will be made on sacks not returned to the Railway Executive.

boxes, when loaded, had possibly been dispatched from a larger station or by road. The railway was a convenient way to deal with bulky but light items that did not bring in much revenue. I can remember that, as a 16-year-old clerk, if the phone rang, which wasn't very often, it would be a local firm requesting that two or three empty boxes be collected. The phone was very ancient, being of the 'candlestick' type with a separate earpiece.

STATIONS IN INDUSTRIAL AREAS

Sometimes the proportion of goods traffic could be quite high in relation to passenger and parcels traffic. This would be the case in the more industrial areas, and it must have been a borderline decision as to whether a separate Goods Agent was required; the title Station Master/Goods Agent was often used. At some stations a fair number of staff were involved with warehouse work, including storage, and a Checker would record inwards and outwards traffic and deal with wagon labels. At Rothwell near Leeds there was a Goods Agent and a small goods yard, while a short distance away, at Robin Hood, there was an SM. Effectively

these two local managers covered the same geographic area, the Goods Agent being responsible for freight and commercial contact with local firms, while the SM covered operating duties. There were no passenger activities except for a few privately hired excursions in the summer. Places like Cleckheaton and Shipley had Goods Agents located at busy goods depots quite close to the passenger stations, each with its own SM.

At Elland there was no passenger traffic except for trains passing through. The operating work included three signal boxes and a fair amount of shunting, but the main reason for the SM job was the power station, with four or five trains of coal arriving each day, a Checker to record the details, and two clerks to deal with the paperwork. Surprisingly, where MGR power stations were involved, the paperwork was less per train, as an MGR train was dealt with as a train rather than each wagon being marked off individually on the advice note, as at older power stations such as Elland. However, the sheer number of trains at, say, Drax counterbalanced this from a clerical point of view and included work in clearing up situations such as a wagon being detached en route. Clearly, whatever the size of the power station,

These platforms at Canonbury station on the North London Line will have seen far more goods than passenger traffic; large numbers of local goods trains passed through, many heading for the docks. No 47497 is seen at 2.20pm on 14 August 1956; note the 'target' number on the buffer-beam to help staff identify the trip number. The old passenger station was later demolished, but a busy electric train service still calls at the other part of the station, to the right.

the SM had to ensure that the trains were kept moving in and out.

At some goods yards A-type and B-type containers were dealt with. These predated Freightliner containers by many years and, of course, required handling by crane, some being mobile ones. There could be problems if a mobile crane had to be moved from one station to another as they were not, generally, licensed to run on public roads. The solution, of course, was for a crane to be towed by a lorry. This was all very well until traffic lights were reached, at which point they might become separated, particularly if the towing was more in word than in deed.

Loads Inspectors would be called in if there were exceptional loads requiring examination. An SM with heavy freight responsibilities would ensure that trains, booked to pick up traffic, cleared all wagons allocated to that service. Extended transits and 'bunching' of traffic (ie too much traffic for one destination at one time) were other matters to be monitored.

The yard might include a lorry weighbridge, in many cases for coal traffic. In rare cases there were rail wagon weighs, generally for scrap metal. Cattle sometimes had to be fed and watered en route, as well as other cattle arriving or departing at the station. Cattle wagons, and many other types, had to be cleaned out after use.

Coal drops, staithes or chutes – there were several names for them – were often used for unloading coal, particularly in the North East. The 3-ton 'cob', or

An up express, the 10.00am Leeds Central-King's Cross with 'A4' No 60006 *Sir Ralph Wedgwood* in charge, is passing through an area of industrial activity on 4 November 1961. Lofthouse Colliery and slag heaps are in the background and there are considerable numbers of empty coal wagons in the sidings on both sides of the main line. Even if the SM had no staff located at a colliery he would be very much involved in the train working and traffic arrangements.

'mechanical horse' as they were also known, was often to be seen, and these vehicles served the railways for many years, long before today's version, the articulated lorry, often of huge proportions, came onto the scene.

This is just a brief glimpse of the type of small goods depot supervised by an SM. In earlier times, before the 1950s/'60s period to which most of this book is devoted, there were huge amounts of other traffics even at fairly small country stations, some seasonal but all serving the community in the days when rail was king.

UNUSUAL AND LITTLE-KNOWN OPERATING MATTERS

To conclude this chapter detailing the duties and responsibilities undertaken by SMs, here are some lesser-known occurrences, which represent only the tip of the iceberg for the railways as a whole.

A platelayer working near Oakenshaw on the Midland main line observed a train approaching from the south. There was a large cloud of dust towards the rear of it, so he flagged the train down. The dust was due to a wagon that was derailed – had it not been for this prompt action there would have been considerable damage at the junction a few hundred yards ahead.

At Arthington South signal box in the 1940s there was a speed check device that the signalman could activate – an approaching train would cause holes to be punched in a tape in the signal box. Depending on the number of such holes it could be seen whether the train was exceeding the speed limit for that stretch of line.

No doubt there have been a few cases over the years of freight trains departing before the brake-van has been attached. This happened at Stanningley and the train was stopped at the next station, Bramley, as the signalman had been advised by phone that the brake-van and Guard had been left behind. In a similar incident near Chester the guard was left behind but caught up with the train and his brake-van by the simple expedient of boarding a local bus, together with his shunting pole and brakestick.

Many years ago, in thick fog and darkness, the Bradford portion of the down 'Yorkshire Pullman' was given the wrong road at Holbeck High Level. The driver stopped quickly but had gone over the points towards Wakefield. It was decided that it was unsafe to set back so the traincrew were requested to proceed via Ardsley and Dewsbury. Unfortunately on the severe gradients of the Dewsbury line the train slipped to a stand on two occasions. The damp conditions made things worse, but a banker was sent to assist each time. The weary passengers and traincrew didn't arrive in Bradford until after midnight, but safety, as always, was the overriding factor and the necessary rules had been observed.

On another occasion not far away I observed a failed DMU complete with passengers being propelled by 'J50' tank loco No 68908. There were many diesel failures in the early days, and in this case the best was made of what was available. I once had to use a Class 47 to propel a Newcastle-Bristol train from Ferrybridge to Moorthorpe due to loco failure. It was a time-consuming business with irate passengers wanting to know what was causing the delay. All you can do in this sort of situation is explain what is happening and that safety is being observed on a line with quite heavy gradients to contend with. At Leeds Central in the 1950s it was normal practice for the locos of some incoming trains to propel the empty stock out of the station, then gravity brought the stock back into the station under the control of the guard.

Vandalism has become a problem over the last 40 years or so – before that it was comparatively rare. Particularly at risk, in the 1960s, was empty stock stabled in sidings; sometimes this was excursion stock stored at an out-of-the-way location for several months. It could also happen when a train was on the move. One Sunday at Castleford a returning excursion from Blackpool was reported as having hooligans rampaging through it near Preston. Unfortunately the person who reported it identified the wrong train and, on arrival at Castleford, the Guard said that there had been no trouble at all on his train.

Five other incidents at Castleford are worthy of brief mention. Vandals used to decorate the inside of the brake-van that was kept overnight in the goods yard. The shunters naturally complained about this, so my Assistant SM and I decided to set a trap on a dark evening and we actually caught one of the offenders. I could run a lot faster in those days! The local police administered a good telling-off, which seemed to do the trick.

One of an SM's fears was realised one Sunday morning when the Assistant SM was on duty for a well-booked excursion. The driver had presumably not read his notices properly and failed to stop. Some of the passengers got away on the next train, which was a 'Garex' private party train, although its organisers were none too happy, having paid for their own train.

About this time, 1969, I saw my first fully fitted freight train minus brake-van, as well as an experiment with loco headcodes whereby the four-digit code had the normal white and black reversed.

The final incident at Castleford illustrates that not all of an SM's tribulations took place on railway property. I had to travel to Leeds by bus on the one occasion when I was a member of an interviewing panel to fill a booking clerk vacancy. Halfway there the offside front tyre blew out. As I and the other decidedly shaken passengers got off it was clear that the offending tyre was completely bald and this was on the very first day that MOT tyre regulations were introduced, for cars at least.

At Pontefract Baghill a private firm was using the goods yard for several months to unload trains of bitumen from Stanlow for use in the construction of the M62 motorway. They were surprised to see a train arriving one day when it was not expected. It turned out to be the previous day's empty train, which had got as far as Tinsley and had then been sent back in error as a loaded train. This would not have happened when TOPS was introduced a few years later. The old, crude method of banging on the side of a wagon to see if it sounded empty would not have been of any use for most types of wagon by the time of this incident.

A strange case regarding bona fide luggage occurred at a station not far away. The local newsagent complained that his business was being adversely affected, allegedly due to a schoolboy returning each afternoon by train with a parcel of evening newspapers that his father then sold locally. Was this legitimate luggage? The case was so unusual that we put it to Divisional Office to sort out.

One day at East Leake a down 'Ord' (local passenger train) arrived somewhat late – this was unusual on the GCR main line of course! A passenger handed me fourpence out of the window and asked me to phone his wife to say he would be late. The train then restarted before I had a chance to say that BR would pay for the call. In these days of mobile phones and compensation to passengers, that sort of event seems very quaint.

Lime was an apparently innocuous substance carried in great quantities by rail. However, it could be a problem if overheated. The answer on at least two occasions of which I heard was to take the wagon to the nearest loco water column for a thorough dousing.

At Tees Yard, late one evening, it was apparent that a very important chemical train from ICI Haverton Hill would have to be cancelled as the only air-braked brake-van was defective. As it was dangerous traffic, a brake-van was required for the guard to travel in. Fortunately we had a pair of air-braked brake-vans at Tees, which were adapter-fitted to couple to 100-ton iron-ore tipplers if they were defective and had to be moved to a repair location. These tipplers had rotary couplers so the vans had to be attached front and rear. When not required the vans languished for weeks in Tees Yard, coupled together. The use of this pair solved the problem, except that we had to ensure that we got them back again.

In October 1960 I was travelling on a Rochdale to Bolton DMU and there was a delay at each station, which was annoying to traincrew and passengers alike. The reason was that, amazingly, the DMU had strayed a long way from its usual haunts on the Western Region. It was apparently common practice on that Region for passenger stock to have door handles which had to be turned when you closed them rather than having a spring mechanism that just involved slamming the door (hence the term 'slam door stock'). The delay was due to the guard having to ensure that all handles were correctly turned before leaving each station.

Single-line working (SLW) was mentioned above under the heading of derailments. I should like to mention just two incidents if only to show that the simple diagram in the Rule Book was, of necessity, a straightforward example of how SLW should be implemented,

explaining the use of detonators and red flags or lamps, the clamping of points, and signals to be kept at Danger, as well as the people involved and many other items. The branch off the Midland main line to Grimethorpe Colliery and Coalite Plant was double track. One track had a large hole in it after a derailment had been cleared up, and a further complication was that another line went off to Goldthorpe MGR bunker from a junction between the main line connection and the location of the blockage. Grimethorpe desperately needed several trains in and out after half a day with no services; coal came in to Grimethorpe for the Coalite Plant and empties were required for coal and Coalite dispatches. Using a modified version of SLW I was able to run the job all night on my own. The use of a signal telephone to Cudworth signal box, which was about 2 miles away and was responsible for the points and signals in the area, enabled me to decide events. There were points to be clamped for each inwards train and priorities to be decided if a Goldthorpe train was expected. Effectively the job was simpler having just one person in such a makeshift and, possibly, unique situation.

Some years later I similarly worked SLW on another night on my own at a location further north, although the circumstances were very different. Generally an SM would implement SLW and, sometimes, be Pilotman as well.

On a lighter note, I had only one instance of a communication cord being pulled, by a rather dignified lady who thought she was on the wrong train leaving Nottingham Victoria. She heard an announcement that the train was going to Aylesbury, and as she was going to East Leake this did not sound quite right.

It was sometimes difficult for an SM to make the decision, in the case of snow and icy weather, to ask the local Ganger to take his men off their normal jobs and transfer to snow and ice duty. Nowadays we have much more reliable weather forecasts, but in those days there could be a difference of opinion as to how the weather was likely to change over the next few hours or, especially, overnight. If it was bad already and likely to deteriorate, the first priority was to keep points and other equipment working. Point heaters were in the future so far as many smaller stations were concerned.

The subject of gongs, bells and whistles sounds rather unlikely in the context of an SM's duties and responsibilities, but they were just another area where an SM might have to know about the equipment and the methods of working in his area. How did they work? Were they safe? How were his staff involved? What should he do in the event of equipment failure? Many of the unusual incidents were completely unique, but others had to be dealt with 24 hours a day, seven days a week. 'During fog or falling snow' will be a very well-known term to anyone who has taken a Rules & Regs exam, and the aforementioned gongs were a great help in such conditions as well as in their normal context of, among other things, assisting in ensuring safe shunting methods. In particular, if regular shunting took place at a location where, due to track curvature or obstructions of one sort or another, the shunter or guard was unable to give the driver the normal hand signals, another method had to be used. An ideal solution, which was used on the GCR main line, for instance, was to have an extra fixed signal. On this line it was regular practice for a whole train to be set back clear of the main line into a siding. If the trains were of a reasonably standard length, the loco would be at or near a point where the extra signal was located, and the signalman could clear this when the points were set. Elsewhere

another method sometimes used was for the signalman, from his higher vantage point, to relay the hand signal from shunter to driver.

Rule 117 in the Rule Book gave the following codes of audible signals to be given to drivers during shunting operations, using bell, gong, horn, whistle or other appliance:

One: go ahead
Two: set back
Three: stop
Four: ease couplings

The Sectional Appendix gave numerous examples of where these codes were used, or where special ones were in use, for example at Gordon Hill where an electric gong affixed to a signal post instructed the driver to set back to the up bay (one beat), to the up main (two beats) or the down sidings (three beats). Likewise, at Manton Wood there was a loud bell operated by the signalman with three set-back codes for particular routes, while at Newark Up Yard there was a gong operated by the shunter for set-back moves into the yard. A further variation was at Grimsby New Bridge, where an electric gong was operated by the signalman but only after the guard had confirmed to him that the points were properly set.

In Yorkshire there were several interesting versions of the principle. In one tunnel gongs were provided to warn drivers of signals just outside the portal; in the days of smoke-filled tunnels these devices must have been well worthwhile.

On the Nostell to Staincross line an electric gong warned drivers that they were approaching a steep downhill incline; it was located by the side of the line 100 yards from the summit. In Dudley Hill Tunnel there was a loud gong to control setting-back movements, the Guard operating the plunger.

2
RELATIONSHIPS
WITH OTHER STAFF

Having looked at some of the duties of an SM, we now need to see the roles of his staff and the SM's relationship with the next level of authority – District or Divisional Office, which I shall refer to as District Office, as the re-organisation that brought in Divisions was in 1964, not very long before the SM's job disappeared.

An SM, like any other manager, needed staff to assist him in carrying out his duties. The number of staff and types of job varied tremendously depending on the size of station and the range of traffic. From the early days of the railways the SM was responsible for the management and safe, efficient operation of the station. There was much mention then of maintaining discipline, keeping staff busy and ensuring that they were punctual when starting duty. He should encourage new entrants and junior staff to become proficient in their jobs and, in due course, work their way up. A clerk could become a manager if he was diligent; even a porter could eventually be a guard or signalman or, perhaps, an SM.

We have seen that, at a large station in the 1950s and '60s, there would be a separate Passenger & Parcels Agent (PPA) to look after the commercial work, leaving the SM to see to the operating, train running and platform side of things,

while at a small or medium station the SM would cover everything. Because of this situation I think it would be relevant, later in this chapter, to have a look at a PPA's duties at a larger station – I have chosen Hull Paragon – because even though the PPA had a different title, he was very much involved in what the passenger would regard as an SM's work. In this context, certainly at a larger station, the role of SM became somewhat blurred so far as the public were concerned. He was a prominent figure, but, as with operating duties, a concept unknown to most of the public, there is a need to clarify the large station organisation.

SUPERVISED STAFF:
PLATFORM AND SIGNALMEN

It is unnecessary to recount in detail the duties of many of an SM's staff, although perhaps two types merit a brief description as they were those most associated with the general view of the SM's work. Porters were very important at one time, and although they do not feature very much in today's railway, other platform staff under new titles do. Signalmen, from the earliest days as 'Policemen', have always figured prominently in the SM's day. Though not

Above This teatime Ashford-Tonbridge stopping train on 22 June 1957 has just terminated and there is considerable activity on the platform. Traincrew and platform staff are getting ready to move the empty stock out of the station to clear the line for the next arrival.

Below Carriage cleaners were among the many staff supervised by an SM. On 11 April 1958 long brushes and buckets are in use by these cleaners in a siding next to Cambridge station's long through platform.

Above A BR loco is in charge of a train of Metropolitan coaches at Aylesbury on 30 April 1961. Note the door windows with their leather straps; these were in use for many years on British trains for the purpose of closing the windows.

Below At the other end of the country, at Craigendoran on 18 June 1959, this West Highland line train has terminated and the porter is carrying out his regular duty of closing the windows by means of pulling up the leather straps.

One of the regular Salisbury-Waterloo trains departs from Whitchurch (Hampshire) headed by 'Battle of Britain' No 34049 *Anti-Aircraft Command*. On the platform some porters are in charge of large barrows. Note the trap points at the end of the loop line protecting the main line.

generally seen now, as signal boxes are fewer and in the background, they certainly still have a vital role in the running and safety of the railway.

SMs also supervised guards, shunters, inspectors, foremen, ticket collectors, signal lampmen, carriage cleaners and several other types of staff.

Porters

A porter's duties were many and varied over the years, even though he was one of the poorest paid members of staff. Often, especially at a small station, he unlocked and locked the station as he was the only person on duty early and late. Sometimes for this reason he might book more tickets than a clerk who was on a middle turn. He attended to the trains and handled parcels, newspapers and mail, including delivering urgent smaller parcels or freight items (freight was normally known

as goods until fairly recent times). Passengers, including the disabled, were also looked after.

There was always a lot of cleaning to be done. This was not easy in the days before sparkling white terrazzo floors and the modern facilities in use at many stations today. As well as general cleaning there were windows, lamps and platforms, including whitening the edges of the latter – then add to this tickets to be collected, posters to be put up, gardening, winding of clocks and the use and securing of platform barrows.

There might be work in the goods yard – shunting, loading and unloading of wagons and working a weighbridge, including charging the customers, often coal merchants. To conclude this list, which is far from comprehensive, there were winter duties such as lighting fires in waiting rooms and staff accommodation and maybe fires for loco water columns. Clearing ice and snow from platforms and sanding the edges, replacing gas mantles and filling fire-buckets with sand in winter and water at other times were important duties.

Generally, during the immediate post-war era, stations could be rather drab due to austerity and the effects of smoke. It was a question of trying to keep on top of things and the porter certainly had a large part to play. Today's stations are, generally, much more acceptable to passengers – and need to be due to road and air competition – and the same applies to the trains, of course.

In the season racing pigeons were very important in some parts of the country, and maybe a few baskets of the birds had to be released for training flights with the time and date recorded on the label before the baskets were sent back to the owners.

Only authorised persons were allowed into the inner sanctum of the signal box. *John Ryan collection*

Sometimes whole trains were used for large competitive races.

A porter-signalman would have normal porter's duties together with opening the signal box for, possibly, a short period each day. There could be a single-line token or staff to be exchanged with the driver of each train, and the SM sometimes did this type of work on a regular basis. For example, at Rushcliffe Halt the porter-signalman opened Hotchley Hill signal box for about 2 hours each afternoon, while the other porter assisted the guard of the two trains that called at the gypsum sidings, and dealt with the wagon labels. The remainder of the men's shifts were spent on platform, parcels and ticket-issuing duties.

Signalmen

What an SM should check for on his routine visits to signal boxes has already been described (see page 20). This is not the place to examine the different types of signal boxes, signals, types of block working, signalmen's general working instructions or the required knowledge of Rules & Regs, but as regards the SM's relationship with signalmen there are a number of points that may be of interest. First, there was a strict rule of no unauthorised access to the box, and there was usually a sign saying 'PRIVATE' on the door.

Phones: The railways had a considerable internal phone system, and it was unusual for a signal box to have a GPO phone. Usually the signal box phone had an internal BR number, enabling the signalman to ring other such phones over a large area. Many signal boxes had so-called 'omnibus' phones with buzzer codes, which enabled all signal boxes or other locations on a particular circuit to listen in at the same time. The codes indicated to whom a call was directed, or maybe it was directed to a group of people for train regulation purposes and reporting the sequence of trains. There would also be a link to District Control in the overall pursuit of keeping trains running to time. The signalman had a lonely job, particularly on nights when it was unlikely that there would be any visits from S&T or Engineer's staff. Guards and crossing-keepers had similarly lonely jobs, but at least signalmen and crossing-keepers had phones to keep in touch.

Level crossings: There were, and still are, many types of level crossings, and some were at stations next to the signal box; this was the traditional type of crossing, but not seen so often nowadays. Some were out in the countryside where a road crossed the line, or were perhaps merely farm crossings. Some were manned, some not. I should like to mention just a few items, as supervision of crossings was, in many cases, very much part of an SM's job.

In some countryside areas a house was situated next to the crossing where a reasonably quiet road crossed the line. The crossing keeper was often a lady, who lived in the house, and the gates were kept closed across the road until a vehicle needed to cross. This might be 24 hours a day or just a two-shift line open between 6.00am and 10.00pm. There were no

Above The 'omnibus' Control Office phone circuit for the Hawkesbury Lane-Coventry-Leamington line, dated April 1962, showing the various buzzer codes. *WA*

Above right and right The classic level crossing location at the platform end beneath the watchful eye of the signalman at Congleton, Cheshire, and the more rural location of Worsborough Dale near Barnsley. *Both John Ryan collection*

signals to be worked by the crossing-keeper but there was a cabin for relief staff, for rest day, holiday or other requirements.

In some cases, after resignalling had taken place, a former signal box would be retained if located at a busy road crossing, with a so-called 'slotting' arrangement whereby the power signal box, maybe many miles away, would signal a train but the signal would remain at danger until the crossing-keeper turned a switch after he or she had lowered the barriers. He had a track diagram, similar in some ways to that in a signal box, and was thus able to see the progress of an approaching train.

One of the old rules about level crossings referred to the lamps. After sunset or during fog or falling snow, lamps must show a red light in each direction along the line when the gates were closed across it, as well as to approaching road traffic when closed across the road. The lamps must be lit as soon as dusk fell.

The block shelf: On the signal box block shelf, in addition to the block instruments, there were bell tappers, the use of which could often be heard on the station platform on a warm day with the signal box windows open, and the block bells even more so; in a busy box they often had different tones to help identify which was ringing. Various repeaters might also be in use, for example to show the position of an out-of-sight signal arm – 'on', 'off' or 'wrong'. The latter indication would require corrective action by means of the signal wire adjuster. Signal lamp repeaters were also sometimes in use.

Train regulation: Some signal boxes had train regulation responsibilities. For example, when I was SM at East Leake the nearest box that carried out this duty was at Loughborough Central. Each train

should go forward onto a stretch of line, in this case to Nottingham, without it or a following one being delayed. Various terms relate to regulation, and the definitions I have date from about 1960:

- Headway: a distance headway is the minimum gap between a train and the following one to enable the latter to run without interference, while time headway is a corresponding time gap, and depends on gradients, speed restrictions, stops at stations, curvature of the line, etc.
- Margin: an interval (time or distance) required between trains running at different speeds to enable them to run without interference from one another.
- Line Capacity (LC): the number of trains that can pass over a stretch of line (consisting of several signal boxes and block sections) in a given time. LC is reduced by having long block sections, and would be improved by making all the sections equal, even more so if the sections were shortened, the speeds of slower trains increased, or maybe Intermediate Block Sections introduced, as was the case between East Leake and Loughborough. This enabled more of the heavier up freight trains to run, in particular the Annesley-Woodford 'Runners'. Other factors involved are general signalling arrangements, physical limitations, gradients, etc, any intermediate facilities for recessing trains, and the varying speeds of trains.
- Line Occupation (LO): the actual number of trains passing over a given stretch of line in a given time. Line Availability was the difference between LC and LO, ie the unproductive use of the line.

District Control was involved in train regulation in conjunction with signalmen

Signal box interiors: the upper photograph is probably of a box at Horbury on the L&YR – note the block shelf with its block instruments above the lever frame, the stove and chimney breast, the wooden stool and armchair, and the Train Register Book desk with telephones and clock – while the other is somewhere on the North Eastern Railway. *Both John Ryan collection*

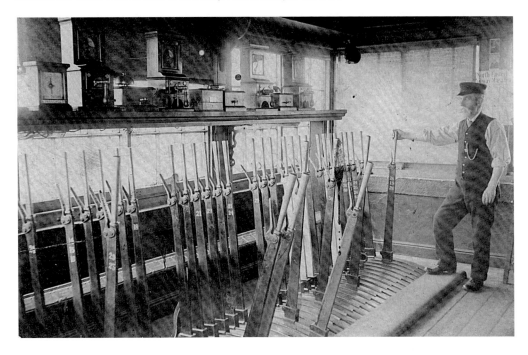

at the regulating signal box, and clearly the SM was also involved, particularly on a busy main line. Mr J. A. K. Gray, District Operating Superintendent at Nottingham Victoria and also my chief when I was at East Leake, had an obvious interest in such matters within his District, and once asked me a question on the subject of train regulation during a visit to East Leake signal box.

Train booker/signal box lad/booking lad: There were many names for this junior member of staff, and he had an important role. He was usually employed at larger, busier boxes, and among his duties were to complete and maintain the Train Register Book, answer the phone, and clean the box and its windows. The lad was even known to operate the white (out-of-use) signal levers until he realised that these did not, in fact, clear the smoke from the tunnel!

Relief signalmen: Although often based at a local station for pay and admin matters, these were frequently under the control of District Office, as they would sometimes have to cover jobs in other SMs' areas. This might be rest day relief, with a regular roster of turns to be covered at the same boxes on a routine basis. In other cases it could be General Purpose (GP), covering vacancies, holidays, sickness, etc. Often the District Signalmen's Inspector (DSI) would ring to ask the relief signalman to go to a particular box for 6.00am as the regular man had phoned in sick, or there could be some other emergency. Whatever the reason, it was a case of keeping the trains moving, and the SM was sometimes involved in these arrangements. Relief signalmen were experienced men with an important role. Their pay included such things as walking time and travelling time to get to and from particular boxes, which

were all agreed with the local staff representatives.

Finally, in this account of signalmen and their work, I would like to include the following extract from *Railway Memories No 6* by Stephen Chapman and Peter Rose, published by Bellcode Books in 1994. It concerns Harold Wainwright, who retired in 1993 as principal of British Rail's operations training centre at Webb House, Crewe, having begun his railway career at Wakefield Kirkgate in 1954. In the late 1940s his relief signalman cousin sometimes worked at Wrenthorpe West box.

"'Like all signal boxes then, it had an atmosphere of smoke, steam, oil, metal polish and paraffin. Other characteristics were the tall desks with high stools, wooden armchair held together with signal wire and padded with well-worn cushions, polished lino floors, burnished lever tops, bright golden brasswork, coal fires, flag sets, oil lamps and strings of detonators."

After joining the railway Mr Wainwright underwent the training and exams necessary to be a signalman before being given his first, temporary posting at Locke's Sidings.

"I will never forget my first shift alone. The responsibility was awesome, but with over 90 moves a shift one didn't have time to worry. Traffic passing Locke's included trans-Pennine expresses, three-coach locals and all kinds of freight. The rising gradient was quite steep on the down and the sight and sound of a 'B16' lifting a Healey Mills to Teesside freight away from a check at the home signal was not to be forgotten."

Aspiring to become a station master, Mr Wainwright moved into the clerical grades and joined the District Operating Superintendent's office at Wakefield Westgate. Following a Station Master's course and successful application for such a posting he moved away from the area in January 1957.'

I have included this extract as it describes, far better than I could, the signal box of the 1940s and 1950s.

SUPERVISED STAFF: INSIDE

We saw in the previous chapter that an SM had responsibilities and duties regarding booking office and parcels office work, including doing some of the work himself at smaller stations or checking the work of others. There are a number of other items to be mentioned in this context. The SM and the booking office staff needed to have a good knowledge of timetables, and he and many other people had copies of the Working Timetable (WTT). These gave more detail than the public timetable, including for example passing times at intermediate points where trains did not call – and times were to the half-minute. All non-passenger trains were shown in addition to the trains known to the passengers from their version of the timetable. We shall see later that some of the official books of Rules & Regs are referred to as, for example, Appendix to or Sectional Appendix to the Working Timetable. Booking clerks to this day need to know the timetable nationwide as well as, of course, whether the trains are running to time, and today's computer systems assist considerably in this.

In the past *Bradshaw's Guide* was indispensable to regular travellers – it is thought that the first one was published in 1838. To Sherlock Holmes and Dr Watson, later in the 19th century, it was needed to plan their journey when 'the game was afoot'. By 1898 Bradshaw ran to 946 pages. There were many other local guides, for instance the *West Yorkshire ABC Railway and Bus Guide* priced at 1 shilling in 1961. Travel agents sold a lot of railway tickets on a commission basis, while on the railway itself the Information or Enquiry Office, later known as 'Travel Centre', originated in the early 1920s at larger stations when it was found that an office separate from the booking office was needed.

At larger stations there were also Left Luggage and Lost Property Offices, and the Telegraph Office was a feature at stations for many years. A telegraph service was provided by railway companies long before Post Offices took over, and was also used extensively for internal railway business from as early as 1839. From 1852 the 10.00am GMT time signal was transmitted throughout the country to enable clocks to be synchronised. In 1870 the GPO took over the public telegraph service, but railway messages continued to be carried free of charge, and I can remember sending many such messages – the ubiquitous email arrived many years later! Women were increasingly employed in railway telegraph offices: in 1900 Edinburgh Waverley had 40 lady telegraph operators sending out 4,000 messages a day.

The 10.00am time signal is received at Rugby Station box (GCR) on Saturday 23 January 1960. *WA*

On a similar subject, the railways had a considerable system of internal mail for railway business. It still sometimes seems strange having to affix a stamp to an envelope, as I must have sent thousands of BR free letters over the years, as well as parcels. Stores and full wagons of goods would also be sent 'Free on Rail', as it was known.

Claims and general public complaints, whether passenger, goods or parcels, were part of an SM's work as well as that of his staff. Claims could involve parcels subject to theft or damage or not arriving at their destination for other reasons. Claims Inspectors dealt with the more important items, but locally the SM would visit customers to inspect damaged goods at their house or a firm's premises. There were lighter moments to this, of course. Sometimes items damaged in transit would be sold off to defray costs. However, if it was, say, tinned groceries, the labels would have been removed and you did not know what you were getting except that it was something made by the firm in question. There were the inevitable claims forms to be filled in and sent to the Claims Office. My uncle worked in one such office, in Leeds, towards the end of his 50 years on the railway.

From earliest times SMs dealt with passengers at first hand, and one of the first rules in the Rule Book was that he should promptly report complaints made by the public. Obviously in many cases he could deal with such complaints very quickly himself and ensure that his staff

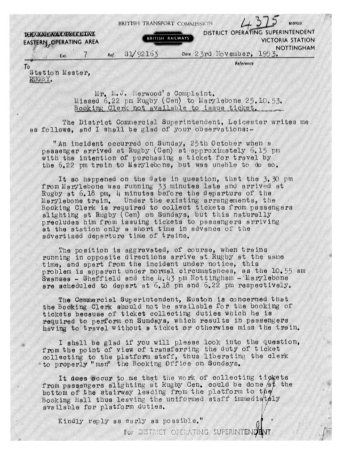

A letter from the DOS at Nottingham Victoria station regarding a prospective passenger's complaint at not being able to purchase a ticket at Rugby Central station – a serious matter that clearly needs the attention of Station Master Potts. WA

Mr Potts advises the landlord of the Coach & Horses Inn at Ashby St Ledgers that a package has arrived for him at Rugby Central. WA

LONDON & NORTH EASTERN RAILWAY.

Ref **RUGBY CENTRAL** Parcels Department, Station,

PARCELS ADVICE CARD

No 2030

April 11th 1919

The undermentioned Merchandise consigned to you has arrived at this station. Kindly arrange for its disposal. On the expiration of one clear day after delivery of this notice or after the time when it should be delivered in the ordinary course of post, the Merchandise will be held by the Company, not as Carriers, but as Warehousemen, and if not taken delivery of on or before........................

Storage Charges will be made.
No credit will be allowed except by special agreement.

From	No. of Articles.	Description.	Approximate Weight lbs.	Charges TO PAY. £ s. d.
?	One	Pkge	44	

PLEASE PRODUCE THIS CARD WHEN MERCHANDISE IS APPLIED FOR.

LNER 403/1/47—200,000

J Potts Agent.

did the same, making sure that customers received the consideration that they, rightly, expected.

If there was a small goods office to be supervised, the SM would check on such items as hand-written advice notes to customers to say that traffic had arrived for them; there were free-of-charge periods for unloading. Also to be checked would be hand-written bills to customers for fixed and excess space, especially for coal storage, demurrage (detention) charges for wagons, storage of items in warehouses, and cartage (collection and delivery) charges. The SM would oversee, generally, the accounts and sign month-end returns.

The station cat was a feature at some places, particularly if there was a goods shed with storage of grain. I can remember there being a milk allowance for these useful creatures, whose job was, of course, to reduce or eliminate rodents. I don't know if station dogs had an allowance, but some were well known many years ago for carrying charity collection boxes. Another dog would appear when a train was due to depart, bark, then disappear until the next one was due! Yet another rang the station bell when a stopping train approached. Conversely, passengers' dogs could, occasionally, cause problems. One

King Charles Spaniel who was accustomed to going to dog shows by train was left behind one day by his mistress. He escaped from the house by jumping out of a window, ran half a mile to the station and dashed into a 1st Class compartment, where he complacently seated himself between two lady passengers. Fortunately the SM, seeing and recognising the dog, sent him home safely, though crestfallen and disappointed.

Freight Rolling Stock (FRS) returns or Wagon Distribution was another element of the work of a small goods office. District Office expected to receive, by a certain time each day, details of surplus wagons and extra wagons required of the various types. The SM ensured that correct types, according to traffic, were used and not hoarded. Wagon Distribution was one of the main reasons for the introduction of the TOPS computer system, and I was a member of the team that implemented the system throughout the country. Only a modern computer system could provide an effective method for using the optimum number of wagons – there were too many built-in delays under the old system of phone or telex messages from one level up to another of the organisation. There were also too many opportunities for

GREAT WESTERN RAILWAY.

ELECTRIC TELEGRAPH DEPARTMENT.

Audlem Station, *Feby 4* 187?

TRUCK REPORT.

PREFIX.

McCorquodale & Co., Printers.   W. G. Code Time _____ No. _____

CLASS OF STOCK.	Broad Gauge CODE SIGNAL.	NUMBER.	Narrow Gauge CODE SIGNAL.	NUMBER.
Van—				
Loaded	V L		V L N	
Empty	V E		V E N	
Wanted Additional	V W		V W N	
To Spare	V S		V S N	
Open—				
Loaded	O L		O L N	2
Empty	O E		O E N	1
Wanted Additional	O W		O W N	
To Spare	O S		O S N	
Cattle—				
Loaded	C L		C L N	
Empty	C E		C E N	
Wanted Additional	C W		C W N	
To Spare	C S		C S N	
Six-Wheel—				
Loaded	S L		...	
Empty	S E		...	
Wanted Additional	S W		...	
To Spare	S S		...	
Covered—				
Loaded	W L		...	
Empty	W E		...	
Wanted Additional	W W		...	
To Spare	W S		...	
Timber—				
Loaded	T L		T L N	
Empty	T E		T E N	
Wanted Additional	T W		T W N	
To Spare	T S		T S N	
Hoppers—				
Loaded	...		H L N	
Empty	...		H E N	
Wanted Additional	...		H W N	
To Spare	...		H S N	
Goods Carriage Trucks—				
Loaded	G L		G L N	
Empty	G E		G E N	
Wanted Additional	G W		G W N	
To Spare	G S		G S N	
Sheets—				
On Hand	Y L		Y L N	2
Wanted Additional	Y W		Y W N	
To Spare	Y S		Y S N	
Hoops—				
On Hand	P L		...	
Wanted Additional	P W		...	
To Spare	P S		...	

Delivered at Telegraph Office ___ m. ___ m. Signed ___

This Report was dispatched by me at ___ m. ___ m. to ___ Station.

___ Clerk.

This Return to be made up and sent from Telegraph Stations to the Carriage and Wagon Inspector by 6.0 p.m. every evening, and from small Stations by Train.

Three open wagons and two sheets are reported at Audlem station in this 7 July 1872 Carriage Stock Report – note the telegraphic code for the status of each type of vehicle or item. WA

people to over-order or hoard wagons and not declare surpluses. The traditional pick-up goods delivered and collected your wagons, loaded or empty. At some small stations there might be just one or two wagons on hand, but they had to be declared under the old system.

In addition to the normal stock there were special wagons, for example shock-absorbing wagons for loco firebricks or plasterboard. Many wagons were in circuit working, such as the 13-ton capacity hopper wagons for gypsum from Rushcliffe Halt to Bletchington (Oxfordshire) for the cement works. There were also some temporary arrangements, as when the M1 motorway was being built, when a stone train ran from Buxton to Dewsbury each day using normal 16-ton common-user wagons. As these were unloaded by grab it meant that some stone was left in each wagon, but it made sense to send the empty train back each day for the next load rather than clean out and return the wagons to normal coal use.

Other outside staff

Shunters: These could be either passenger or goods. At larger stations the passenger shunter would work with the station pilot; this was a feature at all large and many medium-sized stations for many years. Sometimes several pilots were in use. I remember, particularly, the North British tanks at Edinburgh Waverley shunting passenger and parcels stock. Shunters were instructed not to use shunt poles for pinning down wagon brakes – this was a dangerous practice as the pole could break under the pressure used. It was an expensive business as well, replacing broken shunt poles. Brake sticks were provided for the purpose and these were of the correct length and thickness to do the job. At Pontefract Monkhill a shunter was provided mainly because

Above Almost all large and many medium-sized stations in the days of SMs had pilot engines to do the shunting of parcels vans and passenger stock. The Peterborough North station pilot, No 69540, rests during the afternoon of 27 February 1960 while a porter is kept busy with large quantities of parcels and boxes. The number of telegraph wires is quite remarkable.

Right No 69022 is the pilot at Darlington on 16 February 1957. Note the spotters on the up main platform and the 'A5' tank engine on the 12.40pm train to Saltburn.

Right No 55203 undertakes pilot duties at Glasgow St Enoch on 16 June 1959. St Enoch closed many years ago and this photograph is a reminder of the sort of station working arrangements for which an SM had responsibilities at larger stations.

Above No 82010 leaves Exmouth with the 3.36pm train to Exeter Central on 1 July 1960. Above the first coach can be seen a lampman carrying out his duties at the home signal for trains coming off the Budleigh Salterton line.

Below These signals and lamps at Radcliffe-on-Trent are relatively easy for the lampman and S&T lineman to reach; note the telegraph wires attached to the post. No 67787 approaches with the 1.36pm Grantham to Nottingham Victoria train on 14 March 1962. There were still a few ex-GNR somersault signals in use in the mid-1980s.

several coal or coke trains each day had to reverse direction en route between Glasshoughton and Healey Mills, and having a shunter there to assist the guard considerably reduced the time taken to reverse the trains.

Lampmen: At one time an eight-day lamp was in use for signals. Within eight days, effectively weekly, each lamp had to be refilled with oil, cleaned and serviced generally, including attention to wicks. A lamp-room with appropriate fire-prevention arrangements was provided where the lampman had his supplies of barrels of oil, pourers, etc, and a suitable surface on which to place the lamps. He would carry two lamp sticks, each with six full, serviced lamps, climb the ladders, often very high, and change over new for old. The signal spectacles, lenses, reflectors and glasses had to be kept thoroughly clean. Fifty lamps could be a normal day's work, and the distances to be walked had a bearing on this. An SM was expected to check on a routine basis that signal lamps were showing a good light when he made his out-of-hours after-dark visits to signal boxes. This was in addition to any Divisional signal-sighting special trains run, again after dark; I once travelled on one of these trains and it was an interesting experience.

Ticket collectors: As well as checking and collecting passenger tickets, the ticket collector had a number of other duties. Platform tickets were a regular feature at many larger stations, enabling people to go onto the platform to meet or see off passengers – and they were a very important item to the locospotter. When I was quite young I would need fourpence to cover a day's spotting at Leeds City station – threepence for the return bus or train fare and a penny for the platform ticket. Countless other spotters would also be there, on the end of the platform, all day. At a penny a time, BR must have received a large revenue over the years when locospotting was such a popular hobby.

The ticket collector and travelling ticket inspectors would clip tickets. Sometimes a keen inspector would be able to spot the fact that a clip had been done on a particular route. Excess fares were collected if a passenger did not have a

An early GWR excess fare receipt for a single journey from Nantwich to Audlem. Note the list of circumstances under which an excess fare was payable. *WA*

ticket or had, for example, continued past the destination shown on the ticket. Any irregular travel, such as via a wrong route, also had to be dealt with. As with all staff at stations or on trains, there would be questions from passengers about train times, late running and many similar matters.

Guards: Goods guards would not usually be under the control of an SM – not in any great numbers, anyway – but at the larger stations passenger guards would be. Their kit consisted of, among other things, red and green flags, watch and whistle, detonators, hand lamp and notices. If on goods work, duties included checking wagon loads, wagon sheets and labels, one on each side of the wagon.

On passenger work there might be value parcels to be signed for and signatures obtained when they were passed on to another guard or station staff. In some areas cash was carried in large wooden boxes on local trains, again to be signed for when handed over at the main station; this was similar to the sealed leather cash bag arrangement for conveying booking and parcels office cash, wages, etc.

In a scene from another age, No 52119 stands at Holywell Junction on the afternoon of 2 June 1961. The guard is walking past the tender to check his train. Note the sparse driver's cab and the containers and wagons of the period.

Guards sorted parcels en route in the guard's van to ensure that parcels were ready to be put off at each stop. He would also compile a journal – a log of the journey giving such details as the number of coaches, parcels vans, etc, making up the train, timings at the various stations and details of any delays; the latter were followed up when the journals were checked at District Office. At one time, in addition to normal parcels, there might be boxes of fish, milk churns and many other items. Mail was very important from the early days of the railways.

To this day, mothers with prams and pushchairs are looked after by the railway and a great many journeys are made as, with better access, today's trains and stations can make travelling easier with young children and do a job that a bus cannot. The guard is there to assist in getting the pushchair on and off the train and to help any passengers needing assistance.

Recently on a return visit to East Leake I met an elderly lady who told me of how she took her young children on the train to Nottingham in the 1930s. The porter always knew when to expect her and would help carry the pram up the steps from the street, and the guard would hold the train for a minute or two if necessary. East Leake, like many other stations, had virtually no car parking facilities, but most people did not have cars and would walk to the station or get a lift there. This continued into the 1960s, but things are very different at most stations today – sadly, though, not at East Leake and the many other GCR stations now closed, but not forgotten.

It was always emphasised that the guard was in charge of the train. Whether a passenger or goods guard, he had to have route knowledge appropriate to the train he was working. If there was no guard available with the necessary route knowledge, or maybe no guard at all, the train would have to be cancelled. In the days when some trains were not partially or fully 'fitted', ie with continuous wagon brakes that could be controlled by the driver or guard, it was not unknown for a guard to remove the tail lamp in cases of emergency. The signalman at the next box would then stop the train in accordance with the rules, as it had not arrived with its tail lamp attached, and might therefore have become divided in the section. Obviously this type of incident was very much a last resort but necessary to ensure the Safety of the Line.

In this brief account of just a few of the duties of a guard, mention should be made of arrangements for working down steep inclines. The Sectional Appendix gave lists of such inclines and the exact point where the guard or, perhaps, another member of staff had to pin down the wagon brakes. The point where the brakes should be released was also shown. In some cases there were further instructions about the number of brakes to be pinned down.

Number-takers: When I had my first interview for a job on the railway, while still at school, there was brief mention that my job might be as a number-taker. This sounded marvellous as I assumed it meant taking the numbers of locos! This was not, of course, the case, but involved the recording of wagon numbers. I actually started work as a clerk and heard no more about number-takers for some years. When I was SM at Castleford I had a travelling number-taker/checker who recorded wagons arriving and departing at various locations. These included the local goods yard, private sidings (ie those owned by customers) and other places. He was also involved in the labelling of wagons, which included putting details of destination, commodity, etc, on two labels, one for each side of each wagon – label clips were affixed to the wagon for this purpose. Collecting labels from incoming wagons was also part of the job.

Number-takers were not required at the many collieries in the area due to the documentation arrangements in force with the NCB and CEGB, but a coking plant would have a shunter or checker to record details of inwards coal traffic. Many years ago a colossal amount of number-taking was needed if it was required that traffic passing from one railway company to another had to be recorded.

LARGE PASSENGER STATIONS

I would like to describe two examples of large station work. During the period 1964-65 I was able to observe, in detail, the work of the SM and his staff at Newcastle Central and that of the Passenger & Parcels Agent (PPA) and his staff at Hull Paragon. As a Management Trainee I was in the unique position of being able to observe all the many facets of the work, even though I was not involved directly in doing any of the duties, except on one or two occasions.

Newcastle Central, 1965

At this large station there was a total staff of 420 staff in the wages grades with office staff in addition to this. Those 420 were employed in 33 types of jobs, the largest numbers being 122 passenger guards and 78 leading porters (parcels), and they had to cover three shifts a day, seven days a week. There were 21 carriage cleaning staff, in addition to those at Heaton Carriage Sidings, which came under a separate manager. A list for 1901 shows 479 staff, but this appears to cover all station work and all grades, including 11 Assistant SMs, 300 porters and 72 clerks. The 1965 figures are for operating staff including signalmen, but not commercial people, who came under the PPA. Also in 1965 the guards were in ten 'links', and you worked your way up the links in a similar way to drivers. To become a top-link driver or guard was an achievement after many years on the railway, and you might then continue into a supervisory or management job.

Newcastle Central station is in the background of this snowy scene on 4 March 1965. No 65834 is taking water on the avoiding line round the back of the station.

The Assistant SM on each shift covered many aspects, for example overcrowding of trains, public address systems, parcels arrangements on the platforms, mishaps, train punctuality, holding connections and cleaning the station.

Station Inspectors at a large station like Newcastle had a wide variety of responsibilities, including supervision of passenger shunters, movement of parcels, including the work of tractor drivers, and, as always, the punctuality of trains. There were, in addition, parcels, parcels post and ticket inspectors, as well as foremen covering similar areas to the inspectors.

We have seen some of the duties of a porter at a smaller station. At a larger station some of the work was similar, in addition to such jobs as changing tail lamps, dealing with unclaimed luggage, closing carriage windows and dealing with carriage destination boards.

In those days if you asked a member of the station staff for the platform number of your train, they would probably consult a rather voluminous document. This was the daily station working instructions. It showed such things as which platform was to be used by each train, including any extra trains, and engine arrangements, such as whether the loco was to come

from or go to the shed. The District Control Office also made much use of these instructions. The document was produced by the Trains Section under the control of the SM.

The main work of the Station Master's Office (SMO) was effectively a world of its own. In involved the control of the ten links of guards, their daily rosters, use of booked spare men and other associated matters. Again, this was very similar to the work at loco sheds, where driver coverage was needed for normal booked work as well as any eventuality such as staff off sick or trains running late.

The SMO also had Control Order men, and might ask Control for goods guards to cover passenger jobs if needed. At the 'sharp end' was the Time Office, with two clerks on each shift (one on the night shift). Here the guards booked on and off, and there were often last-minute changes to be made for guards' duties and for many of the station staff, too, who were similarly dealt with by the Time Office.

It is often forgotten that, in the days of steam, many main-line and even local trains were moved to and from the station and carriage sidings between jobs: Euston to Willesden was a well-known route, as was Newcastle to Heaton. There were, as there still are, people at main-line stations

Early afternoon at Rugby Midland station in the first quarter of 1966 – a page from *Arrivals and Departures of Passenger Trains*, showing the reporting number, arrival and departure times at Rugby (to the half-minute), the days each train runs, the platform used and remarks about the train and its stopping points. WA

8				WEEKDAYS						
Reporting No.	Time	From	To	DOWN arr	DOWN dep	UP arr	UP dep	Days	Platform	Remarks
1D58	11 25	Euston	Holyhead	13 07	13 15			Dly	1	(1) Holyhead, (2) Workington. Stops at Stafford, Crewe, then Chester, Flint, Prestatyn, Rhyl, Colwyn Bay, Llandudno Jn., Conway, Penmaenmawr, Llanfairfechan, Bangor, Rhosneigr Valley, Holyhead, also Hartford, Warrington, Wigan, Preston, Lancaster, Carnforth and all stations to Barrow, then all stations except Braystones to Whitehaven and Workington.
1A25	09 05	Llandudno	Euston			13 09½	13 17	SX	2	Stops at Northampton, Wolverton, Bletchley, Leighton Buzzard, Watford Jn.
2A88	13 10	Rugby Midland	Euston			13 10		SO	8	EMU. Stops at Long Buckby, Northampton and all stations to Watford Jn.
2B55	12 30	Birmingham	Rugby Midland			13 12½		SO	5	DMU.
1A25	09 05	Llandudno	Euston			13 16	13 24	SO	2	Stops at Northampton, Wolverton, Bletchley, Leighton Buzzard, Watford Jn.
2G54	12 48	Northampton C.	Birmingham	13 17	13 18			Dly	1	DMU. Stops at all stations except Canley Halt.
1A31	06 38	Workington M.	Euston			13L21	13L28	Dly	TL	—
2G55	13 42	Rugby Midland	Birmingham		13 42			SO	5	DMU. Stops at all stations.
1E06	13 43	Rugby Midland	Peterborough East				13 43	SX	7	Stops at Welford & K., Theddingworth WO, Lubenham, Market Harborough, Rockingham, Seaton, Wakerley, King's Cliffe. Stops at Yelvertoft to set down only on notice being given to the guard at Rugby. Stops at Ashley & W. MWFO not advertised.
2B55	12 50	Birmingham	Rugby Midland			13 48		Dly	4	DMU.
1A33	08 39	Carlisle	Euston			13 49½	13 57	Dly	2	Stops at Northampton, Bletchley.
1E06	13 50	Rugby Midland	Peterborough East				13‡50	SO	7	Stops at Welford & K., Market Harborough, Seaton. ‡ 13.47
1A21	11 45	Liverpool Riverside	Euston				13 54	SX Q	TL	—
3A14	11 33	Crewe	Kilburn High Road			14 01	14 46	MX	2	Pcls. Stops at Blisworth, Bletchley.
1F26	12 25	Euston	Liverpool		14 05			Dly	TL	—
2A88	12 10	Euston	Rugby Midland	14 08				Dly	8	EMU.
1S75	13 05	Euston	Glasgow C.	14L39	14L40			SO	TL	—
1S75	13 05	Euston	Glasgow C.		14 40			SX	TL	
1M67	12 24	Ely	Birmingham	14 40½	14 42½			MTh FO	1	DMU. Stops at Coventry, Stechford.
1M67	12 24	Ely	Birmingham	14 40½	14 45½			TWO	1	DMU. Stops at Coventry, Stechford. *
1M67	12 24	Ely	Birmingham	14 40½	14 49½			SO	1	DMU. Stops at Coventry, Stechford.
2K84	14 52	Rugby Midland	Stafford		14 52			Dly	3	EMU. Stops at Nuneaton, Tamworth, Lichfield, Rugeley.
3K07	11 15	Euston	Crewe	14 53	15 23			Dly	TL	Pcls. Stops at Stafford.
2B83	13 55	Stafford	Rugby Midland			15 06½		Dly	4	EMU.

engaged in clearing out the amazing amounts of rubbish left by the travelling public when a train terminates. In those days there was much cleaning by hand of the insides and outsides of coaches. Additionally the shunters at carriage sidings and stations had the job of ensuring that buckeye couplers and buffers were in the correct positions; the buckeyes between coaches were, obviously, coupled together, but those at the two ends of the train should be in the down, out-of-use, position. Similarly, buffers were in the 'short' position between coaches, but were pulled out to the 'long' position, with the 'saddle' applied, at the ends of the train. Trains might also have extra coaches added.

Hull Paragon, 1964/5

Turning now to Hull Paragon, the Passenger & Parcels Agent (PPA) had charge of the Booking Office, Enquiry Office and Parcels Office. The Booking Office was of the traditional type, almost fully enclosed with just the booking

Left 'The Booking Office was of the traditional type, almost fully enclosed with just the booking windows for contact with the passengers.' This undated and unidentified photograph shows the 'business' side of a booking office, with the clerk date-stamping a ticket from one of the many in the racks. *John Ryan collection*

Right and below Passenger receipts for Audlem station, Great Western Railway, amounting to £1 11s 3d, recorded in the Daily Cash Account of Monday 17 February 1868, and the receipt for the money, dated the following day, issued by the Cashier's Office at Chester. *WA*

windows for contact with the passengers. Tickets were issued in large numbers and paid for in cash in most cases; passengers did not then have credit or debit cards. Some warrants were in use, for example for military personnel and other organisations having arrangements with the railway to obtain rail tickets without payment. The warrants were, in effect, cash, and had to be safeguarded so that billing could take place later. The other paperwork in the office, including month-end returns, was familiar to anyone accustomed to booking office work. One difference, however, was the need for a full-time cashier because of the amounts of cash to be dealt with, taken to the bank and cash for wages obtained from the bank. As in all booking offices, the clerks on each shift had to strike a balance before handing over to the next shift. The numbers of tickets sold to each description and their price gave a total debit, together with any other items for which money had been received. Then the cash, warrants or other credit items would be totalled. Hopefully the two sides would balance.

The Enquiry Office was situated at one end of the booking office, open plan and facing onto the concourse. There was no question of someone like me spending a few days just watching the enquiry clerks at work – it was a matter of joining in immediately, particularly at busy periods. A good knowledge of railway geography, seat reservations and a reasonable grasp of the day-to-day fares and conditions of issue of tickets were all assets when thrown in at the deep end. I already had some experience of these matters, but it was a salutary experience and one I never forget when visiting a Travel Centre.

Other facilities included Left Luggage and Lost Property Offices, as well as the many kiosks, vending machines, etc, which, to an extent, were of interest to the PPA. We shall see many of these commercial station items again from a Divisional point of view, as well as the operating aspects of station work.

The Parcels Office at a station like Hull Paragon was of considerable scope and importance. Effectively it covered the surrounding districts of Hull as well as the immediate area, and many collection and delivery vans were in use. Large industrial firms made great use of the parcels service for quicker transits by passenger or parcels

trains, in addition to the accepted slower transits by the sundries service. Sundries were less-than-wagonload traffic by goods train, but again large fleets of delivery vehicles were involved and there was a great deal of transhipment from road to rail, rail to rail, and even road to road.

BRUTEs (British Railways Universal Trolley Equipment) were introduced for some parcels traffic – these were enclosed mesh cages on four wheels containing quite large quantities of parcels for the same destination, and could be towed around large stations. Various types of small containers were also used for goods services, small enough to go into the standard 10-ton van. Conveyor belts were installed at some larger goods sundries depots. As with computerisation of passenger booking, enquiries, seat reservations, etc, and the introduction of debit and credit cards, so on the goods side the abolition of most consignment notes signalled big changes ahead. However, in the mid-1960s there was still a lot of pencil and paper work and expensive manual handling of consignments. Many clerical staff were employed in the Paragon Parcels Office due to the considerable amounts of traffic and revenue involved, and obviously this was even more so at stations larger than Hull; in addition there were Centralised Accounts Offices in large towns dealing with such matters as sending bills to large customers, goods accounts and pay.

On the subject of money, many years ago the SM at a Yorkshire station was surprised to find a half-crown coin (2s 6d) from a Commonwealth country in the booking office cash being prepared for taking to the bank. A less conscientious man might have put it in the bag with the other silver coins and hope that the bank would not notice it. There were, however, arrangements for stations to deal with this. Effectively it involved filling in a form to obtain authority from District Office to take credit for the amount and so balance the books. Half-a-crown was quite a large sum in those days and could not be lightly dismissed as a loss in booking. What the SM probably did not know was the 'paper trail' that this would set in motion from one level of the organisation to another including, of course, the Accounts Department. Each item was small but the total number of forms was later used as an illustration of a need for changing procedures – a far cry from today's computerised arrangements.

OTHER DEPARTMENTS

As well as supervising his own staff and all other staff working at his station, and reporting to District level, the SM dealt on a day-to-day basis with what could be referred to as the technical departments. The dividing lines were not so pronounced many years ago. The local permanent way ganger and Signal & Telegraph (S&T) man were all part of the team, even if under the supervision of their own departments: in GWR days a platelayer lit the waiting room fire in winter at a small unstaffed halt, while in Lancashire & Yorkshire Railway days a platelayer might cover the platform porter's job.

Let us have a brief look at the SM's relationship with these departments. He would have a working relationship with loco drivers, but maybe not with engine sheds, the main Loco or Carriage & Wagon Works or such departments as Outdoor Machinery or the Road Motor Department (Maintenance). Obviously there would be exceptions to this at larger stations or where particular, irregular jobs needed to be done.

Engineer's Department

This could be a confusing term to the public as the word meant engineering in the Brunel tradition, ie building or maintaining the railway track, tunnels, bridges, embankments, the stations themselves and a thousand and one other items.

The local ganger and his staff, in addition to their normal duties maintaining the track and often being involved in weekend work for the larger re-laying and other jobs, had several other duties so far as the SM was concerned. Lineside fences and walls had to be kept in good order. In the days of steam this was the sort of area where there could be problems, particularly out in the country in the summer – lineside fires would spread to fences and adjacent farmers'

'The local permanent way ganger and Signal & Telegraph (S&T) man were all part of the team.' This undated photograph was taken at Madeley (Salop) on the Great Western Railway. *John Ryan collection*

A weedkiller train consisting of No 45268 with brake-vans, a Vanfit wagon, old loco tenders and two coaches, sprays the track beside the wide platform of Armley Canal Road station on 10 March 1964.

fields unless dealt with promptly. As an SM I had dealings with a number of irate farmers because of this. To be fair, I also found farmers to be very helpful in cases where cows had achieved the apparently impossible by getting onto the lineside despite secure fences, gates and thick undergrowth. If it wasn't his cow – perhaps he didn't have a cow with those markings – he would phone his neighbour. This also applied if a cow had been headed off down an embankment, as at East Leake on one occasion, and got through the fence into the wrong field.

We have heard a little about the fogsignalman, who was generally a member of the Engineer's staff. The SM might be involved in taking the fogmen through the required rules before the fog season commenced; certainly, as an Assistant Area Manager, it was one of my regular jobs. Flagmen (handsignalmen) were provided in numerous cases where obstructions were involved, such as when I took over at East Leake and part of the cutting nearby had started to slip. Flagmen were posted 24 hours a day to ensure that the line was safe until a weekend job of clearing the slip could be set up. Single-line working, planned or otherwise, was another example of where flagmen were required.

The Engineer's (Permanent Way) Department often took great pride in maintaining a neat edge to the ballast, general tidiness and the removal of surplus rails and chairs, etc. 'Prize length' signs could be seen from passing trains. The Engineer's Works Department had countless jobs of interest to the SM – station repairs, for example, including painting and plumbing.

Generally the Engineer had to ensure smooth and safe riding for the passengers. As still applies today, vegetation had to be cleared to ensure that train drivers could obtain a clear view forward. Out-of-gauge movements had to start from the planning stage, with Engineers consulting their plans showing structure profiles; from these a route could be worked out using main or slow lines, stabling to let other trains pass and any other constraints. Weedkiller train arrangements were also specified by the Engineer in terms of which lines were to be covered by the train and the strength of the treatment.

Carriage & Wagon Department

At larger stations there were resident C&W staff available to carry out routine inspections and deal with the many last-minute emergencies that could delay the departure of a train, such as door problems, broken windows, defective brake pipes or other brake problems. Nowadays we tend to forget about the difficulties involved in the steam heating of passenger coaches. If there was a lack of heat, was it due to the loco or a defective pipe between vehicles? This was often very obvious on a cold day, when clouds of steam could be seen. At smaller stations contact with the C&W man was often due to emergency situations, and he was certainly one of the people to be called out in the event of a derailment involving passenger or goods rolling-stock.

Signal & Telegraph Department

This department was later known as Signal & Telecommunications. The local S&T technician was another vital member of staff. There was, of course, a great deal of mechanical rather than electrical work at one time, which involved the maintenance and repair of semaphore signals and points with their associated equipment, such as interlocking. Signal wires and point rodding were part of the scene for many years, and there were many defects that could quickly result in delays to trains, so the S&T man, like his Engineer's Department counterpart, was in demand 24 hours a day, seven days a week to keep the trains running. Telegraph equipment in one form or another was around from an amazingly early period of railway history, and as telephones took over they became an increasingly important part of the S&T man's job. As with mobile phones today, it is hard to imagine how the railways would have managed without a comprehensive phone system over the years.

Locomotive Department

Although there may have been little day-to-day contact with loco sheds, the SM nevertheless relied on the quick arrival of the toolvans in cases of derailments. It is no surprise that '4 bells' was the block bell code for a breakdown train or snowplough going to clear the line as well as for express passenger, newspaper or postal trains. The train would consist of a steam crane or toolvans containing jacks, packing, etc. The same cranes would be used on planned weekend jobs lifting parts of bridges, for example. Sometimes more than one crane was needed. On longer jobs particularly, a man on board the train would be appointed to provide hot meals – and woe betide the engine driver who rough-shunted the train when the meal was being prepared!

HIGHER LEVEL: DISTRICT/DIVISIONAL MANAGER'S OFFICE

Although I have previously used the title District Office, as this was the organisation in use until 1964, I shall use the title Divisional Manager's Office (DMO) for this section as most of what follows derives from the 1964-66 period.

From a management point of view the SM reported to the Movements Manager at Divisional level with, of course, important links to the Passenger and Goods Managers. All these officers had numerous sections under their control, and the SM, at one time or another, would be involved with many of them. Going to a higher level there was then Regional Office, in my case the North Eastern Region during its last two years – based at York – and above that came BR HQ at Marylebone.

The work of the DMO was complex and covered a wide spectrum, but I have selected topics that were relevant to the SM, as well as other items of an interesting nature. Some matters were usually determined at Regional or BR HQ level, but with obvious DMO

Occasionally there would be contact with the very highest echelons of the railway industry. This photograph records the visit of the Chairman of the British Transport Commission, Sir Brian Robertson, to Sheffield on 14 March 1958. He is chatting with Motorman Reynolds (left) at Wicker Goods Depot, while Mr W. Scholey, Goods Agent, Sheffield Wicker (right) looks on. *BR*

involvement so far as the SM was concerned. These included national passenger fares, parcels rates, season ticket rates, and public and working timetables, as well as Rules & Regs and Conditions of Service. I have drawn rough demarcations between operating, passenger/goods, and staff (the latter title being used rather than Personnel).

Operating

The hours during which signal boxes were open was a fairly fixed item, apart from weekend arrangements for engineering. Any review to make permanent changes, for example from a box being open three shifts each day to just two, involved the DMO and the SM. As always where signalmen were concerned the Divisional Signalmen's Inspector (DSI) also had a part to play. In addition to taking signalmen through their regular Rules & Regs exams, any permanent or weekend changes to rosters, involvement of relief signalmen or similar matters had to include an input from the DSI. Special instructions applicable to specific signal boxes or level crossings were dealt with by the so-called Outdoor Section (or similar) at the DMO.

The movement of out-of-gauge trains was always of interest. I can remember when the Humber Bridge was being built in the mid-1970s that there was a regular OOG train of steel items from the North East. Essential work was done by the Engineer's Department in working out a route, as has already been mentioned. DMO and Region would then have to send out the necessary notices to all concerned to ensure safe passage of these important trains. General breakdown crane arrangements were also made by the DMO. So far as Rules & Regs were concerned, attention was paid to alterations and interpretation, among other things.

In addition, the following items are associated with this area of the DMO's role: reports of block working irregularities, signals passed at danger, the pulling of communication cords, trains divided, lineside fires, exceeding of speed restrictions, carriage doors left open, animals on the line and, in steam days, excessive smoke from locos. Train accident reports were fully checked and the necessary action taken. If a Joint Enquiry was required – where two or more departments were involved –

arrangements would be made with the requirement for a definite conclusion to be reached. Major accident procedures were also formulated, while Call out arrangements were another important feature, as was fogsignalling. The latter included the agreed posts to be fogged, lists of personnel, and certificates showing that the fogmen had been passed in the necessary exams. All these were authorised by the DMO in addition to the work done by SMs, local gangers and others. Additionally, signal, points or lamp failure reports were dealt with, and reports of damage to crossing gates.

Brake-van census requirements were stipulated, and again we can see that what was a routine matter to the SM may have been handed down by the DMO as a result of, probably, a problem over a much wider area, for example a general shortage of brake-vans or some being put away in a siding instead of being kept in regular use. Trains would have to be cancelled as a result of such shortages, and this was a constant problem for many years. Before TOPS arrived, a census was seen as the best way of dealing with the problem.

Among many other miscellaneous items dealt with by the DMO were extra stops for passenger trains, known as 'special stops'; these were generally one-off occasions and were not shown in the Working Timetable. They were not undertaken lightly, but were sometimes required at short notice for emergency reasons or when delays or cancellations had taken place. The DMO's Control and Traffic Section were involved. Other items included arrangements for pigeon trains; problems such as lack of train heating, late or overcrowded trains, rough riding and lighting difficulties; and lack of 'No Smoking' or shortage of 1st Class accommodation.

Distribution and control of freight and passenger stock was a day-to-day job with SM involvement as well as at DMO, Region and BR levels. Storage of surplus stock may not sound like much of a problem, but a few items should be mentioned. The railways have always striven to provide a passenger service to meet the requirements of the travelling public, both before the days of extensive car ownership and road/air competition and since. Considerable numbers of holiday and excursion trains, including guaranteed excursions, brought with them the problem of storage of stock during the winter. This was often done at smaller stations, as well as at some carriage sidings that were, effectively, retained for all-year storage with busy periods in the summer but not very much movement in or out during the remainder of the year. Coaching stock included suburban non-corridor coaches that were pressed into service at busy times for excursions or even parcels use.

On the freight side there were quite extreme problems at certain times. Heavy industrial areas like Teesside had to keep sidings for storage purposes when the steelworks were on holiday. Parts of old branch lines were also used, in colliery areas too, for pushing down whole trains of empties for a few weeks. This, of course, meant problems due to theft of brasses from axleboxes. At Tees Yard, over the years, it became common practice to use some sidings for storage, if only for a week or two. This was in the days of 'common user' wagons, for example large numbers of steel-carrying or coal wagons, which were stored near to the locations where they would next be needed.

Weekend working for engineering jobs has been mentioned and always figured largely in the work of the SM and the DMO. Liaison was made regarding such items as signal box openings at the weekend, single-line working and pilotman arrangements. I remember one normal weekend activity that was adversely affected by conflicting requirements: a long-welded-rail (LWR) train was booked to replace old with new track on a Sunday afternoon, it was winter and earlier delays meant a late start to the job. Snow then started to fall quite heavily and night was approaching. Requests started to arrive, from Control, for men to go back to their home stations for snow and ice duties – keeping the points clear and similar duties. The manager in charge of the re-railing had no alternative but to order the unloading of the new rails alongside the main line near the sleeper ends and arrange to pick them up and start again at a later date – the LWR train had to be unloaded as it would be needed elsewhere.

Other items under the general heading of operating at DMO level included transhipment of wagons that were defective and unable to proceed further. A crane might be needed to shift the load onto a similar wagon, often at a marshalling yard.

Signal sighting was also very important. Today's electric signals are a great improvement on the oil-lit lamps that needed to be checked to ensure that a good light was shown.

Station equipment, such as lighting and the use of platform barrows, was another aspect to be dealt with, together with many others too numerous to mention.

Passenger/goods

Of particular interest to an SM from a passenger facilities point of view were the following.

The booking office periodically ordered ticket stocks from the printers, but there were sometimes delays, or maybe they were not ordered in time. In those days of the Edmondson card ticket, large numbers bore unique details. There was some scope

for using blanks, with the destination written in, but if you ran out of tickets in daily use it could mean requesting that blank excursion tickets, etc, be used instead of a printed day return.

Warrants for use by public authorities, etc, in lieu of payment by cash for a ticket was a matter for DMO control, as well as higher levels. Cheque problems may seem strange to people nowadays, but debit and credit cards and cheque guarantee cards were unknown then. Most people did not have bank accounts anyway, and there could be problems that a station could not clear without reference to the DMO. Security of booking offices could also be a matter for concern; clearly quite large amounts of cash from ticket sales and parcels traffic, together with wages cash, meant that proper security measures were needed.

Travellers cheques and ticket dating machines were further items of interest. The dating machines had to have a set of metal number and letter types, almost like the old-fashioned printing methods, and there was a need to ensure a good clear date on the ticket. It was very easy to drop the metal date numbers on the floor last thing at night when changing the date ready for early next morning.

A temporary booking office might be needed if rebuilding work was proceeding, and again this would be a job for the DMO to arrange.

Public complaints were an important matter for SMs to deal with, but some items had to be passed to the DMO. It might be a question of damage to a passenger's clothing, a car windscreen broken or any number of similar incidents. Claims and claims prevention were matters of importance to passengers, customers and railways alike. There had to be proper procedures and directives for managers and staff generally to deal with any complaints or claims and to ensure

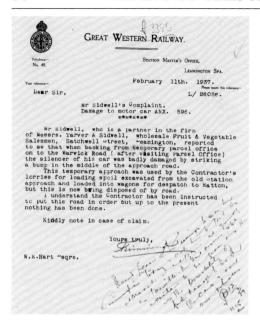

A letter from the SM at Leamington Spa to his superiors in Birmingham warning of a possible claim by a tradesman for damage to his car during the rebuilding of the station in 1936-39. *WA*

that customers felt that their concerns were being addressed and steps taken to prevent similar occurrences.

Travel surveys and passenger censuses were arranged from time to time to ensure that future services met the needs of passengers. A census might take place on a train or at stations.

Seat regulation was a regular feature in the summer, together with normal seat reservations. If you travelled from Paddington on a summer Saturday on a longer-distance service, almost all trains had seat regulation to match the number of seats on the train, and you could not board without obtaining a regulation ticket beforehand. The same applied at many other busy stations in the holiday season. Travelling Ticket Inspectors and Coaching Stock Inspectors (CSI) all had a part to play. The CSIs would be under the control of the DMO and had an important role in checking the

cleanliness and general condition of passenger coaches. It was not unknown for them to be passed out in Rules & Regs and cover for a guard on a short trip to or from the carriage sidings. Horse boxes and special cattle vans (SCV) were then still in use, the latter often conveying pigs.

Troublesome matters requiring action included 'bridge bashes', ie lorries (usually) running into bridges and causing damage. These were not as prevalent then as today, but were still the cause of much delay to trains, including time awaiting the arrival of a BR Bridge Inspector. Trespassing, stones thrown at trains, bills sent to companies that had caused damage to railway property – all were potentially serious and costly matters. Break-ins would involve the British Transport Police, who, even in the 1960s, had cars with radio equipment to enable urgent visits to be made. These, tragically, included more serious incidents on the line, when the SM would also, of course, be called.

Car parks were not quite such an essential feature in the 1950s and '60s, but, together with cycle racks and taxi ranks, were important passenger requirements. At larger stations taxis were required and arrangements were made between the proprietors and BR. Also at larger stations, coin-operated machines, weighing machines, kiosks and shops were all part of the scene, with the SM being consulted about their locations on the concourse.

Not least, on the subject of passenger and freight commercial matters, were BR's sales forces located at the DMO and at higher levels, but this is not the place to go into such a large topic in any great detail. At one time railway salesmen were sometimes known as canvassers, and the duty of canvassing for traffic was part of an SM's or Goods Agent's work. A good deal of advertising of rail services was undertaken by the railways locally and nationally, while the public timetables included considerable amounts of detail about facilities available, as well as the actual train services. An SM had to familiarise himself about all services that were on offer to the public, and maintain contact with the local salesman from the DMO.

To conclude this section, here are a few more items, one-off events in some cases, that illustrate the variety of matters contained in accident reports or in other ways brought to the attention of the DMO so that the necessary action could be taken.

The 'Stop and Examine' bell signal might be sent because of coal falling from a wagon, and the guard would be instrumental in stopping the train. Examination of the line generally was a matter to be reported, together with the results or, in some cases, that nothing had been found. Points might be run through, buffer stops damaged or pushed back, or buffer-locking due to heavy snowfall affecting the line. The use of the 4-5-5 bell signal ('Train or vehicles running away in right direction') might indicate a loco being overloaded. Many of these types of incident would not occur nowadays due to freight trains being fully fitted with air brakes, and loose shunting in sidings being a thing of the past.

The list continues with more mundane, routine, non-accident items: loan of locos to private firms; haulage of private locos over BR tracks; exhibition coaches or trains; sale of loco ashes; fuel for stations and signal boxes; and the sale of railway houses and land. Everyday items included the supply of point clamps and re-railing jacks, provision of clocks and station seats, and dealing with wayleaves. One unusual item was that the DMO had to decide which clock or watch was correct when a delay had been reported, as the guard and station inspector might have given different versions.

Private siding agreements for firms that had their own sidings – sometimes including clauses about the amounts of traffic to be forwarded – were also dealt with by the DMO (private firm's staff came under the control of the SM while on BR property).

Staff

The Staff Office at DMO level was very much involved with putting forward details of jobs to be advertised to the staff. This, of course, included SM posts and all other jobs under the general heading of Traffic Department staff, wages grades, clerical and management. The subsequent application forms had to be processed and interviews arranged. At larger stations the SM could hold interviews for lower-graded non-clerical jobs accompanied by someone from the DMO Staff Office, while the SM could find staff locally for base-grade jobs after first consulting the DMO.

Above base grade, jobs had to be advertised on the Wages Grade vacancy lists. Seniority was an important factor in these grades: signalmen worked their way up to higher-graded, higher-paid boxes, and other staff had similar well-defined routes if they wanted to get on. The situation regarding overtime, 12-hour shifts, rest day working and Sunday working were all part of the equation when deciding whether to apply for promotion – did your present or possible future job include these? The DMO as well as SMs had, of course, to keep an eye on these extra costs, which were often necessary to keep 24-hours-a-day, seven-days-a-week coverage, but needed to be kept to a minimum. In those days some staff continued to work until they were 70, but it was very much the exception.

	(i) Basic weekly rate	(ii) Basic hourly rate	(iii) Annual wages	(iv) Clothing	(v) National Insurance & G.P.S.	(vi) Pension contribution	(vii) Sickness Scheme outpayment	(viii) TOTAL	(ix) Holiday Relief	(x) Annual cost	(xi) Cost per hour	(xii) Annual cost including rest day relief	(xiii) Cost per 8 hour shift
		s. d.	£. s. d.	£. s. d.	£. s. d.	£. s. d.	£. s. d.	£. s. d.	£. s. d.	£. s. d.	£. s. d.	£. s. d.	£. s. d.
COMMERCIAL GRADES													
Porter	211/-	5 0¼	548 12 0	5 17 5	42 13 7	5 17 0	2 3 5	605 3 5	37 1 0	642 4 5	5 11	733 19 4	2 7 1
Leading Goods Porter	218/-	5 2¼	566 16 0	5 17 5	43 15 4	5 17 0	2 3 5	624 9 2	38 4 8	662 13 10	6 1	757 7 3	2 8 7
Craneman	230/-	5 5¾	598 0 0	5 17 5	45 10 0	5 17 0	2 7 3	657 11 8	40 5 2	697 16 10	6 5	797 10 8	2 11 1
Checker	230/-	5 5	598 0 0	5 17 5	44 8 6	5 17 0	2 7 3	656 10 2	40 3 11	696 14 1	6 5	796 4 8	2 11 0
Senior Checker	245/-	5 10	637 0 0	5 17 5	46 11 8	5 17 0	3 4 10	698 10 11	42 15 4	741 6 3	6 9	847 4 3	2 14 4
Timekeeper (Special)	258/-	6 1¾	670 16 0	11 4 9	50 9 6	8 5 0	3 1 3	743 16 6	45 10 10	789 7 4	7 3	902 2 8	2 17 10
Working Foreman	258/-	6 1¾	670 16 0	11 4 7	48 15 0	8 5 0	3 1 3	742 11 10	45 9 4	788 1 2	7 3	900 12 9	2 17 9
Capstanman	230/-	5 5¾	598 0 0	12 17 4	46 11 8	5 17 0	2 7 4	665 13 4	40 15 1	706 8 5	6 6	807 6 9	2 11 9
Tractor Shunter Driver	230/-	5 5¾	598 0 0	11 13 5	47 0 6	5 17 0	2 7 4	664 18 3	40 14 2	705 12 5	6 6	806 8 6	2 11 8
Mobile Crane Driver :-													
Up to 5 tons	230/-	5 5¾	598 0 0	5 17 5	48 15 0	5 17 0	2 7 3	660 16 8	40 9 2	701 5 10	6 5	801 9 6	2 11 5
Over 5 tons to 8 tons	237/-	5 7¾	616 4 0	5 17 5	49 17 0	5 17 0	2 12 11	680 8 4	41 13 2	722 1[illegible] 6	6 7	825 4 7	2 12 11
Over 8 tons	245/-	5 10	637 0 0	5 17 5	51 11 6	5 17 0	2 19 5	703 5 4	43 1 2	746 6 6	6 10	852 18 10	2 14 8
Motor Driver :-													
5 tons or less	230/-	5 5¾	598 0 0	11 9 11	44 17 0	5 17 0	1 11 8	661 15 7	40 10 2	702 5 9	6 5	802 12 3	2 11 5
Over 5 tons to 8 tons	237/-	5 7¾	616 4 0	11 9 11	45 10 0	5 17 0	1 15 6	680 16 5	41 13 8	722 10 1	6 7	825 14 5	2 12 11
Over 8 tons to 12 tons	245/-	5 10	637 0 0	11 9 11	46 11 8	5 17 0	1 19 11	702 18 6	43 0 9	745 19 3	6 10	852 10 7	2 14 8
Over 12 tons	250/-	5 11½	650 0 0	11 9 11	47 0 6	5 17 0	2 2 7	716 10 0	43 17 4	760 7 4	7 0	868 19 10	2 15 8
Road Motor Attendant	218/-	5 2¼	566 16 0	11 4 9	46 11 8	5 17 0	1 9 2	631 18 7	38 13 9	670 12 4	6 2	766 8 5	2 9 2
MOTIVE POWER GRADES													
Driver (Train driving)	328/-	7 9¾	852 16 0	8 18 9	53 10 6	8 5 0	5 4 7	928 14 10	56 17 3	985 12 1	9 0	1126 8 1	3 12 2
Driver (Shunting)	312/-	7 5¼	811 4 0	8 18 9	53 10 6	8 5 0	4 13 10	886 12 1	54 5 8	940 17 9	8 7	1075 6 0	3 8 11
Fireman	278/-	6 7½	722 16 0	8 18 9	51 11 6	8 5 0	3 11 1	795 2 4	48 13 7	843 15 11	7 9	964 6 9	3 1 10
Cleaner	230/-	5 5¼	598 0 0	8 10 5	44 17 0	5 17 0	2 4 5	659 8 10	40 7 6	699 16 4	6 5	799 12 5	2 11 3
Shedman	211/-	5 0¼	548 12 0	3 10 6	42 5 0	5 17 0	2 0 10	602 5 4	36 17 6	639 2 10	5 10	730 8 11	2 6 10
Leading Shedman	223/-	5 3¼	579 16 0	3 10 6	43 15 4	5 17 0	2 0 10	634 19 8	38 17 6	673 17 2	6 2	770 2 6	2 9 4
Senior Shedman	230/-	5 5¾	598 0 0	3 10 6	44 17 0	5 17 0	2 4 5	654 8 11	40 1 4	694 10 3	6 4	793 14 7	2 10 11
Foreman's Assistant III	237/-	5 7¾	616 4 0	3 10 6	45 19 0	5 17 0	2 9 10	674 0 4	41 5 4	715 5 8	6 7	817 9 4	2 12 5
Foreman's Assistant II	250/-	5 11½	650 0 0	3 10 6	47 13 4	5 17 0	2 19 10	710 0 8	53 9 5	753 10 1	6 11	861 1 10	2 15 2
Shed Chargeman Cat. 'C'	245/-	5 10	637 0 0	3 10 6	47 0 6	5 17 0	2 15 11	696 3 11	42 12 6	738 16 5	6 9	844 7 4	2 14 2
Timekeeper M.C.	237/-	5 7¾	616 4 0	3 10 6	45 19 0	5 17 0	2 9 10	674 0 4	41 5 4	715 5 8	6 7	817 9 4	2 12 5
Storekeeper	237/-	5 7¾	616 4 0	3 10 10	45 19 0	5 17 0	2 9 10	674 0 8	41 5 4	715 6 0	6 7	817 9 9	2 12 5
Chargeman Engine Cleaner	250/-	5 11½	650 0 0	3 11 6	47 13 4	8 5 0	2 12 3	712 2 1	43 12 0	755 14 1	6 11	863 13 3	2 15 4
Loco Shed Head Shunter	265/-	6 3¾	689 0 0	12 9 9	49 17 0	8 5 0	3 2 4	762 14 1	46 13 11	809 8 0	7 5	925 0 7	2 19 4

Annual and hourly costs for Traffic Department wages grade staff, as issued by the Traffic Costing Service, York, in January 1965. *Author's collection*

The railway Medical Officers had, of course, a very important role in the recruitment and ongoing employment of staff. An example might be if a job was being advertised due to the person who normally did the job being off on long-term illness. Personal accidents to staff had to be investigated and followed through. From as early as the 1850s railway staff had to be passed as medically fit and also had to have the ability to read and write.

The provision of DMO-controlled relief staff was clearly of interest to SMs. Relief SMs' pay arrangements and rosters, as well as control of relief porters, signalmen and clerks, were all essential DMO responsibilities, again, to keep the '24/7' industry going and ensuring that adequately trained and experienced staff with, where necessary, the appropriate Rules & Regs knowledge were available.

Other aspects covered by the Staff Office included uniform clothing, welfare arrangements, staff accommodation and canteens. The Staff Suggestion Scheme and the First Aid class requirements were other important items. Finally, commendations to staff who had dealt with difficult incidents must be mentioned. It is still the case to this day, as reports in *Rail News* confirm, that incidents beyond the normal course of duty are recognised, as are people doing their normal day-to-day duties to a very high standard and being much appreciated by the passengers. Again this is part of the tradition of the railway world and the railway family.

CONTROL OFFICE

On leaving school in 1954, this was where I wanted to work. Our local spotters club had arranged an evening visit to the Control Office at Leeds City, and I also had a brief visit to the much smaller

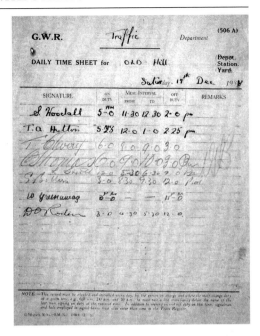

The Traffic Department Daily Time Sheet for Old Hill station, GWR, on Saturday 17 December 1938. *WA*

Control Office at Leeds Central. The idea of earning a living by monitoring all the trains passing through the District, and recording details of loco numbers and goods train loads, seemed too good to be true. Constant telephone contacts with signal boxes, stations, marshalling yards and engine sheds – what more could a railway enthusiast wish? The railways had suffered a great deal while providing essential services during the war, but huge efforts were being made to get back to the sort of services required by the passengers. In addition, at a time of full employment it was difficult to fill jobs in an industry where wages were lower than in some others and there was a lot of shiftwork. You had to start at the bottom at 16 in, maybe, a goods office or booking office. I never did work in Control as my career took me to the SM side, but certainly both were part of the nitty-gritty of the railways.

A typical Control Office set-up would consist of some or all of the following elements, which might vary in different parts of the country – Train, Traffic, Freight, Passenger and Loco. The senior man on each shift was the Deputy Chief Controller (DCC). The geographic area of the Division for Control purposes would be split up; for example, in the case of Newcastle it was divided into sections known as North Main Line, South Main Line, and so on. A Loco Controller and his assistant, a Freight Controller and his assistant (because of the high volumes of freight), and a Passenger Controller made up the other jobs in the office, giving a shift total of 12, including the six Section Controllers and the DCC. Section Controllers covered train and traffic functions as well as participating in other matters for which there were specialist Controllers in the office.

Briefly, some of the duties covered were as follows.

Section Controllers

The Section Controllers recorded movements of trains on graphs, using different colours for different types of train – passenger, freight, etc – and taking reports from signal boxes on the progress of the trains. They were involved with 'margins', as mentioned above when dealing with signalmen's duties, and with brake-van balances with the Scottish Region. One way to describe these balances is to mention the method used on the former GCR main line. Because there were more up 'Runners' (Annesley-Woodford) than down trains coming back, there was a resultant imbalance of brake-vans, so some down trains included extra vans being sent back to Annesley. (The imbalance was due to the up 'Runners' being mainly heavy coal trains but coming back mainly empty wagons, so fewer trains were needed.)

The Section Controllers recorded details of wagons on hand at selected locations, traffic control being in the form of arranging services to pick up traffic. They also kept signalmen advised, in advance, of the order of trains along a main line; recorded punctuality of trains and details such as signal failures; and dealt with freight trip working arrangements.

Freight Controller

This member of the team had control of freight loco working, local trips, etc. He recorded traffic on hand at main marshalling yards; arranged to move traffic after a train cancellation, or fluctuations in traffic; and arranged 'back loads' for any extra trains coming into the Division.

Passenger Controller

The Passenger Controller made arrangements regarding outwards services after a late-running incoming train – connections, special stops, punctuality, passengers stranded, diversions, conductors required for traincrews with lack of route knowledge, etc – bus substitutions, keeping station announcers informed of problems, and DMU arrangements.

Loco Controller

This Controller checked what each loco was doing, or if it was in for repairs. He matched locos to trains to ensure that all were covered, dealt with the effects of late running and loco failures, and checked adherence to loco diagrams (the locos' booked workings). He also checked the road and loco knowledge of drivers and secondmen, ensuring that locos were not sent to Regions where men had no knowledge of that type of diesel or, later, electric loco.

Above The Control Office was involved with local trip workings such as this one, 9J95, headed by 'Q6' No 63363 at Boldon Colliery on 29 October 1965. There was still a good deal of steam activity on freight trains in the North East at that time. An old lower-quadrant signal is highlighted by the smoke.

Below Laisterdyke, near Bradford, seen here on 5 September 1961, represented a typical small local marshalling yard with plenty of traffic to be seen. Ex-GNR 'J50' tank engines such as No 68908 seen here shunted this type of yard in the West Riding over a long period of time; they also worked on passenger and goods station pilot duties, and undertook empty stock and local goods trip workings.

Deputy Chief Controller

The DCC maintained contact with Regional Control regarding extra and cancelled trains and the brake-van position. He gathered details for the DMO morning conference – for example, the position regarding loaded traffic, empties, and loco balances – and also dealt with wagon orders – for example, whole trains of empties from other Divisions.

Control Log

This was always a fascinating document, showing any unusual incidents and call-outs of staff, including SMs, due to emergencies; trains cancelled, with the reasons and any extras run; reports of wagons detached with hot axleboxes; congestion; delays; diversions; loco failures; and many more items.

From all of this it will be seen that there was an important monitoring role for Control, as well as routine matters and reports – when things were running according to plan and conversations with signalmen, etc, were of an advisory nature. It is fine to have a Working Timetable very carefully compiled, together with notices of extra trains fitted into the overall plan. However, things do not always go according to plan, due to weather conditions and many other reasons. Control had to, and still does, deal with emergency situations as well as fluctuations in traffic, together with such things as late running. The SM was often at the receiving end of these sorts of problems and had to rely on Control to make arrangements not only for his area but for surrounding areas affecting him; Control had contact with other Divisional Controls and Regional Control.

Finally, I should mention that manning of shifts varied, some being only two shifts a day, and there were, of course, relief controllers. Many local passenger services were not graphed unless there were problems. Extensive use was made of wires (telegrams) on the internal systems to advise of the make-up of trains, departure times, etc. For freight trains, any perishable or similarly urgent traffic would be shown on these wires.

Much of the telephone communication, for example with signal boxes, was by means of the BR internal system; each controller had a small switchboard identical to the others in the office, but he just answered or called certain circuits, and he could speak to any signal box, station, etc, on that circuit.

Other departments

The SM was not involved very much with Regional Office, not directly anyway. Indirectly many things of interest were decided there. At that level BR had its own architects who, among many other things, were responsible for the design procedures for passenger and staff buildings, including signs at stations. The Chief Civil Engineer (CCE) covered the maintenance of buildings as well as track, etc. Route Availability (RA) was assessed by the Engineers Department; this was very important as it ensured that locos and rolling-stock were only allowed to work over particular lines provided they were in the RA group suitable to those lines.

Speed restrictions were another vital item for the Engineer; for example, after track relaying could the speed restriction be removed at the planned time? Many of these types of matters were decided at District Engineer level.

3
A TYPICAL DAY IN THE LIFE OF A STATION MASTER

This chapter is largely an account of a normal sort of day at East Leake station and Rushcliffe Halt, on the former Great Central main line south of Nottingham. The date is 1962-63, which included the extremely harsh winter of 1963. We shall, however, look at a more normal day from a weather point of view, while acknowledging the special problems of ice, snow and fog in the workings of the railway.

Let us therefore recall a pleasant summer's day at East Leake, where the station was situated half in and half out of a cutting, with the gardens of nearby houses coming up to the boundary fence. The country road from East Leake to West Leake passed under the northern end of the platform and there were steps up from the road to the island platform, passed by trains, almost entirely steam-hauled, on both sides. There was a small goods yard and a signal box. At Rushcliffe Halt there were two platforms and a footbridge, together with a signal box named Hotchley Hill, controlling access to sidings belonging to a firm now known as British Gypsum. My job title was Station Master/Goods Agent East Leake also in charge of Rushcliffe Halt.

Obviously at a couple of small stations like these not all of what one would regard as normal day-to-day station activities occurred. I have, therefore, included a few other items from elsewhere. Many of the SM's duties have been described in detail in previous chapters so will only be mentioned briefly here for the sake of completeness.

Due to the apparently short-term nature of my appointment as SM East Leake, I lived in lodgings in Gotham; the station house at East Leake was not, in any case, available. To an extent these sorts of matters were dominated by the planned closure of many of the stations on the GC main line.

My day started with a short road journey to East Leake station, arriving in time for the main commuter train of the day to Nottingham. The timetable for Winter 1961/62 shows the train as departing at 8.31am. Surprisingly it was the one through train of the day from Marylebone that called here; leaving London at 3.40am, it was mainly a parcels service until it reached Woodford Halse. There were seven other trains to Nottingham Victoria each weekday from East Leake. In the other direction, southwards, the first train of the day had departed at 6.46am, although earlier on Saturdays. By coincidence the last train of the day was at 6.46pm, which meant a 12-

Above The 11.16am Bournemouth West-Newcastle express runs through East Leake cutting on 7 July 1962. A slip occurred here earlier that year; it has been repaired but the grass is yet to grow again.

Below The 5.45pm SX Leicester Central to Nottingham Victoria fast commuter train made only one call, at Loughborough – it is seen running through East Leake on 27 March 1962. The gardens of the adjacent houses made this a very pleasant location. Note the sign attached to the wall of the waiting room announcing that you could telephone from here.

Above No 60961 rushes through the station on 20 February 1963 with the 12.38pm Marylebone-Nottingham Victoria train. Note the lamp case, the fenced area where the road passes underneath and, beyond that, the covered steps leading up from the road to the platform.

Right In May 2002 the platform and one running line survive, and through the lattice fence of the bridge can be seen the bricked-up road-level entrance to the station. *Will Adams*

hour day to be covered, plus time to open up and lock up. The day return fare to Nottingham was 2s 9d, and it took 20 minutes for the 9 miles, including three intermediate stops.

George, the clerk, lived in Nottingham and arrived on one of the early trains, then booked tickets during most of the morning rush, which consisted altogether of three trains each way up to and including the 8.31am. The tickets were of the Edmondson card type, so well known for many years, which were dated using a pillar-type stamper. George dealt with tickets, parcels and the goods work, which was mainly in respect of the gypsum traffic from Hotchley Hill. We shall have a look at the working and staffing arrangements at Rushcliffe Halt later.

The East Leake signalmen's arrange-ments were straightforward, with one man on each of the three shifts covering 24 hours a day for the period from Monday morning to Saturday evening. There were trains going through on Sundays, but the box was normally closed. Relief for the rest days, holidays, illness, vacancies, etc, was provided from elsewhere, as there were no relief signalmen based here.

That leaves the platform staffing arrangements, which were unusual but, no doubt, not unique. There should have been porters on early and late shifts to cover the full train service. However, both jobs were vacant, and there was no point in trying to fill them in view of the apparently short-term future. When I first visited East Leake, arriving about 4.00pm on the through 1.55pm Sheffield Victoria to Leicester Central train just before Christmas 1961, the first thing I saw was a notice of proposed closure. This stated that most of the smaller stations on the GC main line, including both of my stations, would close. In fact, it was to be March 1963 when Rushcliffe Halt closed, and 1969 in the case of East Leake. When I took over on 22 January 1962 there was a temporary arrangement whereby Tommy, a relief porter from Nottingham Victoria, covered the platform duties.

My job in the morning consisted of working in the office, of which there was only one – the booking office. Routine duties included a lot of paperwork. There

In 1962 there was still a regular Sunday service through East Leake, but the trains did not call and the signal box was normally closed. On 10 June No 61056 passes with the 9.30am (Suns) Sheffield Victoria to Swindon train. The siding next to the signal box was used at times for stabling empty wagons.

were no computers or pocket calculators, so it was all pencil-and-paper stuff. This, however, was no different from what I had been doing since 1954.

The pay for the small number of staff – seven, including myself – was all worked out and payslips produced manually. The Engineer's Department wages were worked out by their own department. Other work included ordering uniform clothing, leave and roster arrangements, including any weekend requirements for box openings for engineering work. Rosters included covering holidays and vacancies, etc – District Office supplied relief staff to cover for the porters, the clerk and my job.

Stores, stationery and fuel had to be ordered. This included coal for the signal boxes, office, porter's room and waiting rooms. Paraffin was an important item for the lamps on the platforms at both stations. Stores included cleaning materials with, of course, emphasis on brushes for whitening the platform edges. Snow-clearing items were also very important in view of the severe winter that we experienced.

Rule 33 in the Rule Book stated that clocks at stations and signal boxes must be corrected on receipt of the daily time signal. The second item of Rule 33 is extremely quaint, looking at it today: it says that if the time signal is not received, the SM must obtain the precise time from the guard of the first stopping train that commenced its journey after 10.00am or other specified time so that the station clocks could be corrected. Each guard, when on duty, must satisfy himself that his watch is correct.

The 'omnibus' (open) phone system linking Nottingham and Loughborough was used to report, among other things, the sequence of trains along that stretch of the GC main line. On Summer Saturdays there were considerable numbers of holiday trains on the line, and the information as to how they were running was of interest to all signalmen and stations concerned along the route. The progress of the 'Runners' (Annesley-Woodford freights) was also of interest six days a week.

Some of my routine signal box visits were in the morning to East Leake box and, of necessity, in the afternoon to Hotchley Hill. The required checks were carried out and notices delivered. The times of visits varied a good deal, of course, as they had to be unexpected; this also applied to out-of-hours visits.

Tommy the porter and I dealt with platform duties, seeing trains in and out, closing windows and doors, handling parcels and assisting passengers as necessary. Tommy also made the tea in a large teapot filled from a huge kettle, which had an almost permanent home on the fire in the porter's room. Tommy also did the shunting at East Leake goods yard. This was fairly infrequent as it was basically dealing with received trains of perlite; these arrived from Boston Docks every few weeks and consisted of sheeted wagons containing a material used in the manufacture of building plaster at the Gotham Works. Sometimes the train came through East Leake heading south (up) so that it could then return on the down main to enable access to the goods yard, which was shunted from the north end. After the train had been placed in the yard ready for unloading it was Tommy's job to retrieve a sample bag of perlite from the end wagon of the train. (The 'end wagon' could be at either end, depending on whether the train had taken a different route than normal to reach East Leake, resulting, perhaps, in an additional reversal.) I then delivered this bag to the Gotham Works on the way to my lodgings for lunch. District Office arranged for a mobile crane to proceed,

Above No 61454 brings the 3.10am Dringhouses-Woodford fitted freight train through East Leake at 8.10am on 30 June 1962. The nearer platform building contains the Ladies and General waiting rooms.

Below No 67779 brings the 9.55am Rugby Central to Nottingham Victoria train towards East Leake on 27 September 1962. This was the train that conveyed the pay one day each week. Barnston Tunnel can be seen in the background; you can still travel along this pleasant stretch of line by train from Ruddington or Rushcliffe Halt.

very slowly, from its base at Alfreton to East Leake by road, and a firm of hauliers delivered the perlite to Gotham. The works there had its own siding, which had a daily train service to collect the plaster, but the siding was unsuitable for unloading the perlite. Sometimes I did the shunting of the perlite train if Tommy was unavailable.

Another important job in the morning was a check of the passenger facilities. These included two waiting rooms, one for ladies, and in the winter good fires were kept replenished in both by Tommy. Floors, seats and windows were checked for cleanliness. The waiting area between the steps from the road and the booking office window was an important feature of GC London Extension stations. It was under cover, of course, and had seats, posters and timetables. The only GPO phone on the station was a public phone in the general waiting room, and a bell rang in the nearby booking office if there was an incoming call. For outgoing calls it was a question of waiting until there were no passengers about, taking money from the till and making the call; the money used had to be put through the books to explain the slight shortfall in cash.

At about 11.05am an important train arrived. Hauled by an 'L1' tank engine, on one day each week it conveyed the wages in a sealed leather pouch. The train was the 9.55am from Rugby Central, one of the two daily return Nottingham-Rugby trains hauled by Colwick 'L1s', which also often worked the daily Queens Walk-Gotham freight. Altogether I observed 31 classes of steam loco at East Leake in 14 months. During the morning three fitted freights from York Dringhouses came through, the locos being any combination of classes 'B1', 'B16' and 'V2'.

My trip back to my lodgings for lunch would often be delayed by the 'L1' on the Gotham train shunting over the level

A Wages Receipt Form for a clerk at Rugby Central. Note that apparently the LNER is still paying the wages, just over a year into nationalisation! WA

crossing on the main road adjacent to the Gotham Works. The main traffic from that location was bags of plaster loaded in shock-absorbing vans. However, I was not involved in this, as Tom Little, SM Ruddington, was in charge of the Gotham branch, together with Gotham Sidings on the main line, Ruddington station and the MOD sidings at Ruddington. It was Tom and his wife who lived in the station house at East Leake, where he had been SM until promoted to Ruddington. A charming couple, they were a great help to me in my early SM days. Tom retired in December 1962.

After lunch my next port of call was almost always Rushcliffe Halt. The reason for this was that the goods porter and porter-signalman would be just starting their jobs dealing with the two daily goods trains that served Hotchley Hill Sidings. The porter-signalman opened the signal box for a couple of hours and I would often make a routine visit there. The goods porter assisted the guards of the two trains with the shunting and also dealt with the wagon destination labelling for the gypsum and plasterboard wagons as well as collecting the consignment notes from the firm. These went to George, the clerk at East Leake. My job was to man

Above The 1.07pm Queens Walk to Hotchley Hill gypsum empties are being propelled into Hotchley Hill Sidings at Rushcliffe Halt by 'Royal Scot' No 46112 at 2.26pm on 18 December 1962. Most of the train is comprised of 16-ton mineral wagons, while the three small hopper wagons are for the Bletchington traffic. Note the lamp cases and shelter. The signal on the left at the end of the platform was 'approach lit', ie there was no light until a train approached.

Below Just after 2 o'clock on 23 July 1962 '9F' No 92093 was photographed with the 1.35pm Bulwell to Woodford Halse, a typical up 'Runner' conveying coal. As usual at this time of day I was working in the booking office at Rushcliffe Halt.

the booking office, which was in a small wooden building next to the main road overlooking the station platforms. This gave a perfect view of the '9F'-hauled 'Runners' storming through, mainly loaded with coal going south and empties back.

While there I checked the books, including ticket issues and parcels. Ticket ordering or any similar matters would be arranged. I would carry out the same sorts of checks of the station as at East Leake, although the facilities were more basic, to say the least.

From an operating point of view I had to ensure that the necessary numbers of empty wagons were supplied to the firm. This included 13-ton hopper wagons in circuit working loaded to Bletchington, Oxfordshire, and back empty. I ensured that all loaded traffic was cleared to Annesley (northbound destinations) and Leicester (southbound). Within about a couple of hours of my arrival at East Leake on my first day in January 1962 I met some of the firm's staff at Hotchley Hill gypsum and plasterboard works, as it was important to make sure that the firm received a first-class service from BR each day. That and looking after the passengers and, of course, ensuring Safety of the Line and staff safety would be a large part of my responsibilities from now on.

In addition to visiting the firm at Hotchley Hill I kept in touch by phone regarding such items as a late-running train service for the gypsum traffic. From time to time as an SM I would also visit firms, together with a Freight Salesman from District Office, to discuss requirements.

We must not leave Rushcliffe Halt without having a look at the famous golfing umbrella. I heard several stories as to why Rushcliffe Halt was built, later than the other stations in 1911, and with two platforms rather than an island

platform. One reason suggested was that it was for people going to the adjacent golf course, many of whom would travel by train in the early 1900s of course. A large golf-type umbrella was still retained at the halt even in 1962. What happened if more than one golfer arrived on a wet day was not mentioned!

I could not understand why Rushcliffe Halt was called a halt, as it was fully manned by the goods porter and porter-signalman throughout the day, with booking, parcels and waiting facilities.

Lighting was primitive at both stations, with paraffin lamps in use. It was much easier in the summer, of course, as the stations were open for about 12 hours of daylight. In winter dealing with the platform Tilley lamps took some time in the early morning and late afternoon. Each lamp's mantle had to be pre-heated and it would not light until this had been done. Then pumping sent the paraffin up from the reservoir to the mantle, producing a satisfying popping noise as the mantle became lit. The lamps then had to be placed in the lamp cases on the lamp posts along the platform. In the office the Aladdin lamps had tall glass chimneys and were easier to use. Gas was in use at many stations, for example at Bramley, Leeds, when I was the booking clerk in 1959. I can remember gas being used in private houses in Bramley then and, in the late 1960s, in Castleford. When I was at Cudworth in about 1970 I recall seeing large numbers of the old oil hand lamps in store after being replaced by the new Bardic lamps; the prototype Bardic was tested in December 1962, then modified for full introduction from May 1965.

My efforts in entering East Leake in the Station Gardens Competition consisted of placing hanging baskets beneath the platform canopy. This meant that some were above the platform edges and subject to strong draughts and smoke from passing steam trains. Those nearer the booking office were more successful. At Castleford a large hanging basket in the booking hall met with favourable comments from passengers.

As SM I would deal with any complaints from passengers about late-running trains and, like all other railway staff who spent time on the platforms, would answer questions about train services, fares and delays. The supply of accurate information and reassurance that all is being taken care of are so important to passengers. Obviously at places like East Leake there were not the problems

A letter from the District Operating Superintendent, Nottingham Victoria, to the SM at Rugby Central. It refers to a delay to a freight train recorded by the guard in his journal, and asks for more information from the SM. WA

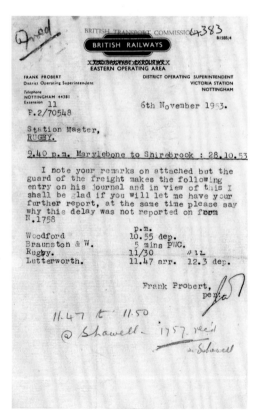

associated with large stations – changing trains, multiple platforms and alternative arrangements in cases of cancellations, etc, then and now, are matters for good management. This was evident, too, in the early days of the railways, and SMs ensured that their staff dealt courteously with passengers' concerns.

Excursions from East Leake and Rushcliffe Halt were mainly to Skegness and Cleethorpes. On 5 August 1962 an excursion to Cleethorpes had a return fare of 15 shillings, and the same year Skegness, Sutton-on-Sea and Mable-thorpe could be visited for sixpence less. Leicester City Transport provided late bus services to meet some return excursions on arrival back at Leicester Central station; this was all part of the commitment to passenger requirements. I can remember late-night buses in Leeds in the 1950s, although these were not in connection with rail services and ran anyway in the days before people had cars. They certainly met a need if you missed the last train from London and ended up on the 9.05pm St Pancras to Edinburgh Waverley, arriving at Leeds at 2.19am.

At East Leake I would carry out checks of the booking office, parcels and goods books and accounts, including signing the month-end returns. On Wednesdays and Saturdays, if I was Off Call, I would have the afternoon off, otherwise I worked all day.

We have seen that, at small stations such as East Leake, the SM might carry out almost any duty from time to time. Often this was due to someone being off work ill or on leave and no suitable relief being available. Booking tickets, answering phone enquiries, dealing with parcels, including delivery of urgent items, and covering the porter's job, including shunting, were all the sorts of jobs you expected to do at times. I did not have to work either of the signal boxes,

The East Coast resorts of Skegness, Sutton-on-Sea and Mablethorpe were popular destinations for excursions from the GC line, both before and after nationalisation. Note the 'late bus arrangements at Leicester' on the BR handbill. *WA*

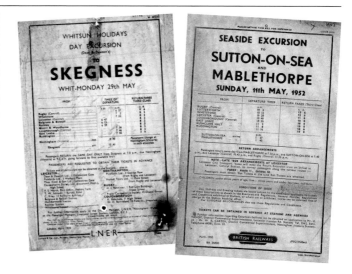

but at Castleford I had that job occasionally. At other stations I also did claims inspections, collected outstanding accounts and read gas, water and electricity meters.

It may be of interest to know the required measurements for station platforms, as in about 1960. The minimum height for platforms was 2ft 9in, maximum 3 feet, and the minimum width 12 feet. They should be long enough for the trains serving the station, have a suitable surface and adequate lighting (presumably some of these requirements were in respect of new or rebuilt stations). Station signs were to be as follows: the main station nameboard was to have letters 12 inches high, on other nameboards letters 3 inches high, while Enquiry Office, Ticket Office, Telegraph and Refreshments were to have 4-inch Gill Sans lettering. Some stations had lower platforms, with a requirement for portable steps or other methods to assist passengers.

Sometimes events out on the line required my attention. There was an Intermediate Block Section between East Leake and Loughborough, and a signal lamp failure one afternoon meant that I

had to warn traincrews of all up trains until the S&T lineman could attend to it. On 13 February 1962 a 'B1' loco shunting a heavy perlite train in East Leake goods yard was unable to prevent the brake-van being pushed through the buffer stops due to the weight of the train and the wet rail. The breakdown crane cleared up the derailment, with some delay as the crane jib obstructed the main line, so the job had to be suspended each time a train was due, which was pretty frequently in those days.

In a country district there were bound to be events of an agricultural nature, including cows and sheep on the line and fires affecting nearby fields as well as railway embankments. Hot axle boxes were another occasional feature on this line, often involving 'Runners' returning from Woodford Halse to Annesley with many empty 16-ton mineral wagons. If an axle box ran hot, clouds of smoke would appear, but the offending wagon would soon be detached and progress resumed.

Back in the office there were sometimes routine visits by auditors or pay auditors. This applied throughout the country and the visits were, of course, unexpected in the sense that you knew they would be

Above It is just after 11 o'clock on the morning of 28 February 1963, and on the right in the goods yard at East Leake are frozen wagon sheets from a perlite train. The empty train has been removed, leaving the difficult job of folding the sheets before they can be sent away for their next assignment. In the background No 48035 passes with the 9.48am Annesley to Leicester freight; '8F' locos started to appear on the line about this time.

Below Another wintry scene at Armley Moor on New Year's Eve 1961, with No 45014 heading the 1.45pm (Suns) Leeds Central-Liverpool Exchange service. The signalman would need his stove on a day like this. Snow and ice brought with them many duties for the signalman and the SM – keeping traffic moving was the main job.

coming to carry out checks but not when. About this time the ball-point pen started to replace the old pen-and-ink method of recording in Train Register Books, and signalmen were expected to sign to acknowledge receipt of their pen and refills.

In winter there were many extra jobs to do. In addition to more time being spent on lighting the station, there were also duties involved with clearing ice and snow from platforms. Rule 22 of the Rule Book referred also to steps, ramps and crossings being treated to avoid accidents by slipping; sand, small ballast or ashes were to be used. Platform edges in particular were very important, while the local ganger and his men had to keep points and other items clear. During the severe winter of 1963 it was difficult for everyone concerned in keeping the traffic moving. Signalmen were instructed to frequently work signals, points, locks and bars when there were no trains signalled, in order to prevent snow and ice from stopping the equipment from working. One train of perlite presented us with another problem. When the sheets were removed from each wagon in turn for unloading they were thrown to the ground, and some froze before they could be properly folded, even during the daytime. In the end it became such a problem that I requested District Office to supply a gang of men to get the job done – the sheets were, of course, urgently required for use elsewhere. Platform barrows had to be kept secure at all times to ensure they were not in the way of passengers or near platform edges.

'WHAT A STATION MASTER SHOULD CHECK'

This list was issued in 1966 from BR's North Eastern Region HQ at York, and showed what an SM should check, some items daily and others as necessary. It is followed by other general comments about how the station should be run in order to provide passengers with the best possible facilities. Clearly both lists refer to the situation at larger stations:

Street signs: are there appropriate signs in nearby streets directing you towards the station?

The exterior appearance of the station as you approach: entrance.

At some large stations staff are employed as Station Guides: are they doing their job properly?

Lighting.

Directional signs and signs generally.

Check booking office, enquiry office and parcels office.

Concourse.

Ladies and Gents facilities, including washing.

Waiting rooms.

Refreshment room.

Station Announcer: what is and what is not being announced?

Destination and arrival indicators: do they show ETAs, late running with explanations, etc?

Litter bins.

Windows and floors: are they clean?

Check left luggage and lost property offices.

Ticket Inspectors: are they helpful and giving platform numbers to passengers?

Check printed departure sheets and amendments to services.

Check flowers, hanging baskets and seats.

Heating.

Check staff are meeting incoming trains.

Check 'Train For' indicators on platforms.

Check staff attitudes towards passengers.

Subways: can be a problem to keep clean and tidy.

Is the station generally clean, light and airy?

The following are general, longer-term items, but some involved regular checks:

The problem of passengers congregating at one point on the platform, boarding the train and walking through searching for vacant seats: this causes delays to trains and inconvenience to passengers.

Where should passengers wait on the platform if they have seat reservations or require 1st Class accommodation?

Hand-written notices: if necessary, are they well written and presented?

Enquiry Office: standards of information supplied and helpfulness to intending passengers.

Seat reservation counter should be separate from casual enquiries.

Vandalism to be dealt with.

Car parks and taxi arrangements to be monitored.

Station Master's Office and Inspector's Offices: are they signed?

Is the name of the SM shown and hours when offices are open?

Concourse generally: is it noisy and cluttered?

Kiosks, adverts, phones: are these suitably located?

Trains with short stopping times to be monitored.

Arrival indicators to show ETA 30 minutes beforehand, but enquiry staff to know an hour before.

Luggage factor: people tend to use trains if staying away overnight, and there is also a large holiday factor with people tending to make just one journey a year.

The remainder of the list is, as you might expect, to do with the need to deal with delays and connections. It starts with the requirement for information about late-running trains and connections, and how to deal with missed connections:

Loudspeakers should be audible and the announcer should seek information about delays, etc, not just wait for it.

Station Guides to meet late trains and supplement any announcements, helping passengers generally.

If train is 20 minutes late, give explanations.

If a local train is more than 10 minutes late, station staff should be told so that they can advise passengers.

If a starting train is delayed by 5 minutes, passengers should be informed by loudspeaker with explanation.

Sometimes even the best public information and signage fails. When I was SM at Batley in late 1967, at a time when Leeds City station was in the throes of

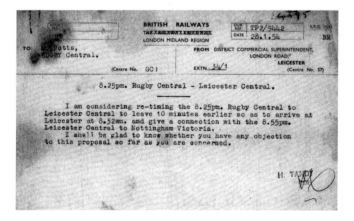

Rugby Central's SM is consulted by the District Commercial Superintendent regarding the re-timing of a down passenger service to provide a better connection at Leicester Central. WA

'THE IDEAL STATION MASTER'

This article appeared in the July 1905 edition of the *Great Western Railway Magazine* and was written by Edward S. Hadley:

'A thousand station masters render service to the Great Western Railway Company. A thousand younger hands aspire to succeed them, and more than another thousand look forward to the attainment of the positions at some, perhaps distant future time. To all of these it is a matter of concern to know what qualifications and attributes constitute an ideal station master.

A station master has much to attend to. His correspondence and other office work take up a great deal of his time, and he has to supervise the work of the clerks in the goods, parcels and booking offices, also of all other men employed at his station. He is expected to pay frequent visits to the signal boxes, daily inspect the station premises, attend to the goods and mineral trains shunting at his station, and when passenger trains are due his place is on the platform to see that passengers get every attention and that the trains are despatched without delay. There are offices, works and shops to be visited, and private persons to be waited upon. The station master is in demand here, there and everywhere, and to give perfect attention to all would almost require the capacity of being in at least two places at the same time.

During the time he manages to get for his office work he has to contend with a succession of interruptions. Persons call for information, or perhaps to complain. Some of the staff come for direction, or the telegraph messenger arrives with telegrams that require instant attention. One pair of hands fails to accomplish what is required of them. The ideal station master should have two.

The station master must possess a store of information. He must know how to deal with every contingency and every emergency. For all kinds of traffic, from timber and coal to bullion and wild animals, he must know the manner of loading and unloading, the conditions of acceptance, the regulations for forwarding and the method of charging. He must know where the company's liability begins and ends in regard to all the matters he may have to deal with. He must be conversant with By-laws, Carriers' Acts, Board of Trade requirements and Railway Clearing House regulations, as well as with hundreds of instructions issued by his own company. Before he can know his business or hope to give satisfaction to his superior officials, he must read and inwardly digest many volumes of rules, regulations and instructions.

Nothing on or about the station must escape the station master's notice. He has to have an eye on the signals, the lines and sidings, the platforms, the lamps, the rooms and offices, the advertisements, the bills and time sheets, the staff at work, and any who may perchance be idle; in fact, he must see that everything is in order, that nothing is done that ought not to be done, and that nothing is left undone that ought to be done. He should be able to look in every direction all the time.

The station master is held responsible for the faithful and efficient discharge of the duties devolving upon all the company's servants employed at his station, and it occasionally falls to him to have to give a word of warning to members of his staff. He must at all times comport himself in such a way as will lead his men to respect his authority, and when he has to administer a rebuke, he must possess the necessary dignity of manner, firmness of speech, and the piercing eye that looks right through the delinquent.

Not every man has these qualifications, and too rarely does one attain them. Fortunately, however, most officers in charge of stations give a good deal of satisfaction while possessing only some of them. If among our readers haply there be one who possesses the whole of the attributes we have mentioned, he should indeed be classed as an ideal station master.'

No 61939 passes Gotham Sidings at 7.38pm on 13 June 1962 with the 4.30pm Grimsby to Whitland fish train. This was one of the two daily fish trains that came through East Leake in the early evening. The first four wagons are conveying containers.

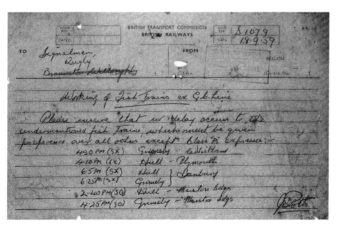

Some three years earlier Mr Potts, the Rugby Central SM, sent this memo to the signalmen under his charge at Rugby and Braunston & Willoughby asking them to ensure that the listed fish trains – including the Grimsby-Whitland – 'must be given preference over all others except Class "A" expresses'. *WA*

extensive rebuilding, we had a few problems, especially during the evening rush hour, when two or three trains would have to depart from the same platform at Leeds, one train following shortly behind the other. Despite the best efforts of the station staff, extensive signage, etc, inevitably some passengers boarded the wrong train, and we had several such passengers arriving at Batley over a period of a few weeks. We would ensure that they returned to Leeds on the next available train.

But let us now return to East Leake as the day draws to a close. If I was covering the porter's job I would stay on for the last train at 6.46pm and lock up. I would sometimes see the two fish trains, perhaps staying until they came through, always a sight worth seeing. The trains were pretty long, one was from Hull and the other from Grimsby, and 'K3' locos were used for both – sadly, just a couple of years or so later this traffic came to an end. There was also a down freight about this time with a 'B16' loco that had gone up during the morning.

The present-day situation at East Leake is very unusual. There is still a single track from the Midland main line at Loughborough to Ruddington, and regular trains of gypsum arrive at Hotchley Hill from Drax Power Station. This in itself is decidedly unusual in that it reverses the original arrangements, up to the 1980s, of gypsum being forwarded, rather than received, by rail. In addition, services operated by the preserved Great Central Railway (Nottingham) from

Cancels Handbill AD136

Train Service

Nottingham Arkwright Street and Rugby Central.

on and from 1 January 1968 the following service will operate.

						SO			SX
NOTTINGHAM Arkwright St.	dep.	07 50	08 22	12 27	13 55	16 17	17 34	18 52
EAST LEAKE	dep.	08 03	08 35	12 40	14 08	16 30	17 47	19 05
LOUGHBOROUGH Central	arr.	08 10	08 42	12 47	14 15	16 37	17 54	19 12
LEICESTER Central	dep.	08 11	08 43	12 48	14 16	16 38	17 55	19 13
	arr.	08 24	08 56	13 01	14 29	16 51	18 08	19 26
ASHBY MAGNA	dep.	08 26	08 58	13 03	14 31	16 53	18 10	19 28
LUTTERWORTH	dep.	08 41	09 13	13 18	14 46	17 08	18 25	19 43
RUGBY Central	dep.	08 48	09 20	13 25	14 53	17 15	18 32	19 50
	arr.	08 57	09 29	13 34	15 02	17 24	18 41	19 59

					SO			SX	
RUGBY Central	dep.	—	07 11	10 30	12 30	15 05	16 20	17 37	18 55
LUTTERWORTH	dep.	—	07 20	10 39	12 39	15 14	16 29	17 46	19 04
ASHBY MAGNA	dep.	—	07 28	10 47	12 47	15 22	16 37	17 54	19 12
LEICESTER Central	arr.	—	07 41	11 00	13 00	15 35	16 50	18 07	19 25
	dep.	07 10	07 43	11 02	13 05	15 37	16 55	18 12	19 30
LOUGHBOROUGH Central	arr.	07 20	07 54	11 13	13 16	15 48	17 06	18 23	19 41
	dep.	07 22	07 55	11 14	13 17	15 49	17 07	18 24	19 42
EAST LEAKE	dep.	07 30	08 03	11 22	13 25	15 57	17 15	18 32	19 50
NOTTINGHAM Arkwright St.	arr.	07 42	08 15	11 34	13 37	16 09	17 27	18 44	20 02

Notes: SO—Saturday only.   SX—Saturdays excepted.

This service will provide SECOND CLASS accommodation only.

Passengers will be able to obtain tickets, between stations served by this Service only, from the Guard in charge of the train.

Accommodation will be provided for the conveyance of cycles, perambulators, etc., accompanied by passengers, who will be responsible for the removal of these articles from the stations.

Unaccompanied traffic will not be conveyed.

Season tickets, between stations served by the Service only, will be issued at Nottingham Midland, Leicester London Road and Rugby Midland Stations.

From:	Notting-ham		East Leake		Lough-boro Cen.		Leicester Central		Ashby Magna		Lutter-worth		Rugby Central	
To:	S	R	S	R	S	R	S	R	S	R	S	R	S	R
Nottingham														
East Leake	2/6	3/9												
Loughboro Central	3/9	5/-	1/4	2/6										
Leicester Central	6/3	7/6	4/3	5/6	2/9	4/6								
Ashby Magna	8/9	11/-	6/6	10/-	5/6	9/-	2/9	4/9						
Lutterworth	9/9	13/6	7/9	12/-	6/3	11/3	4/-	6/3	1/2	2/3				
Rugby Central	11/9	16/-	9/9	14/6	6/3	14/3	5/6	9/-	3/-	5/6	2/-	3/9		

The return fare quoted above is that for Cheap Day Return.

British Rail
London Midland Region

Issued by British Railways Divisional Manager, Furlong House, Middle Furlong Road, Nottingham.

AD136X   BR 35000   December, 1967

East Leake became an unstaffed halt in September 1966 when the former GCR London Extension was closed south of Rugby. A 'paytrain' service between Rugby and Nottingham Arkwright Street survived until May 1969, when this remnant of the once important main line also finally succumbed.

Nottingham Transport Heritage Centre at Ruddington, some steam-hauled, run from Ruddington to Rushcliffe Halt and, sometimes, further south towards Loughborough.

4
OFFICIAL PUBLICATIONS

'**R**ules & Regs' was a general term used to cover an SM's knowledge of the required books of instructions. He had to ensure adherence, by his staff, to the sections relevant to them. Some books were partly of a descriptive nature, for example telling you how the vacuum brake worked. Many other railway staff needed to know the Rules & Regs concerning their duties and had to be competent and pass exams, often oral, to ensure that everyone involved with Safety of the Line was up to date. The SM had to pass exams on a regular basis and he and many other people attended classes, particularly before the initial exams. Many people found it worthwhile to continue classes and so build up a comprehensive knowledge.

As always there were enthusiastic people who, recognising the need to learn, then became keen to become competent in every possible aspect. For some, such as District Inspectors, it was a way of life – they had to know the rules inside out and put them into effect out on the line. They also took the SM, signalmen and many others through the periodic exams. You knew what to expect if you fell in for an exam with the keenest inspector whose knowledge was positively encyclopaedic. For many staff it was

gaining one of these skills, together with the practical side of the job, that was so important: it set them aside from others and was something of which they could be proud. This also applies to many jobs outside the railway, of course.

There was a great deal to learn and keep up with, including numerous amendments. Later, books of a modular type were introduced so that a whole section could be replaced rather than the old method of sticking in strips of paper or writing in some of the smaller items.

This is not the place to go into the history of how the vast number of instructions were built up by the various railway companies. It would also be inappropriate to give more than a brief summary, but it should include some of the more interesting items. Even in my time in the 1950s and '60s there were instructions to be observed by traincrews of one BR Region when working over another – for example, speed restrictions. This highlights the fact that there were, very broadly, two types of items in the books.

BR's nationwide rules of a general nature were to be observed by all, and they followed on from whatever arrangements the 'Big Four' private railway companies had before 1948.

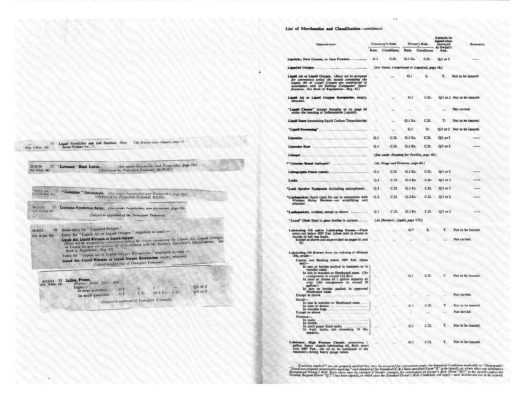

Above The SM and his staff had to keep up to date with amendments to all sorts of rules and instructions, and this late-1940s Book of Rates for Merchandise by Passenger Train has the opposite page blank so that amendment slips can be pasted in. WA

Below BR Telegram forms normally included code words to reduce the total number of words to be transmitted by the Telegraph Office. WA

Below Preface of the Standard List of Telegraphic Addresses, issued by the Railway Executive in 1952. WA

PREFACE

The standard postal and railway abbreviated telegraphic addresses which are set out in this publication operate from the 1st April, 1952, from which date all other methods of addressing telegrams will be cancelled.

Particular attention is called to the procedure to be followed in the case of Railway and Postal Telegrams as set out below :—

RAILWAY TELEGRAMS.

Abbreviated Railway Telegraphic Titles.

When sending Railway Telegrams to addressees not included in pages 4 to 24, the following abbreviations must be used instead of inserting the full name :—

e.g., Mr. Smith, Goods Agent, Newtown, would be G Newtown

and a multiple message to the Station Master, Goods and Parcels Departments, Newtown, should be addressed as under :—

SG & P Newtown.

DESIGNATION	ABBREVIATION
Goods Office	G
Ticket Office	B
Parcels Office	P
Lost Property Office	LPO
Lost Property Depot	LPD
Station Master	S
Refreshment Room	RR
Yard Master	Y
Left Luggage Office	LLO
Police	POLICE
Station Hotels	HOTEL
Control Offices	CONTROL
Telegraph Lineman	TELINE
Signal Lineman	SIGLINE
Motive Power Depot	LOCO
Telegraph Office	TELE
Carriage and Wagon Depot	CW
Outdoor Machinery Depot	ODM
Road Motor Depot	RM

STATION	ABBREVIATION
Aberdeen	ABDN
Beattock	BEATK
Birkenhead	BHEAD
Birmingham (Snow Hill)	BHAM S H
Birmingham (New St.)	BHAM N ST
Birmingham (Lawley St.)	BHAM L ST
Birmingham (Central)	BHAM CENT
Bishopsgate	BISGATE
Bristol	BSTOL
Burntisland	BURNT
Cambridge	CAMB
Cardiff	CDFF
Carlisle	CLSE
Carstairs	STAIRS
Darlington	DTON
Doncaster	DON
Dumfries	DFS
Dundee (Taybridge)	DUN TB
Dundee (West)	DUN WEST
Dundee (East)	DUN EAST
Dunfermline, (Upper)	DUNF UP
Durham	DHM

1

Secondly were the more descriptive items, such as train heating arrangements and countless local instructions showing methods of working. Obviously there were rules to be followed in these cases too.

Telegraph codes

This was not a book of rules, although the preface stated that the codes, each representing phrases in regular use, should only be used internally within BR, not in messages to members of the public sent via the GPO. In the days when huge numbers of messages were sent by telegraph, it was necessary to keep things as brief as possible while still putting over exactly what needed to be said. There were sometimes important safety elements, such as in the case of out-of-gauge loads.

To the older railwayman the book is pure joy. You might find a telegram form (not actually sent) on your desk if you were late back from lunch, perhaps reading 'CHIK Fred' (or whatever your name was). The code word 'CHIK' meant 'Following missing, urgently wanted. Have special enquiries made and if with you forward immediately and reply.' I hasten to add that messages actually sent by telegraph, or the later teleprinter, telex or TOPS, were of a strictly business nature.

Many codes concerned train working and restrictions on the acceptance of freight, etc. Passenger trains had a section, which included 'Adex', 'Mystex', 'Footex' and 'Halfex', each describing different types of excursion train. A message containing the code word 'Warnpass' would be sent to all concerned advising of problems on the line at a particular location, when passengers needed to be warned of possible delays or diversions.

Other codes of a general nature included 'Falcon', 'Walnut', 'Amber', 'Arrow', 'Kale' and 'Derwent', all of which had specific meanings and helped to keep messages short. Although at one time free of charge when sent by GPO, it was obviously important to keep messages concise.

Regulations for Train Signalling and Signalmen's General Instructions

The title gives a very good clue as to the contents; it was very much a signalmen's book and therefore relevant also to the SM. As with so many other books, it is possible to see how methods were built up over the years. The history of signals, block working and train braking systems is well worth studying by the railway student: Absolute Block, Permissive Block, Train Staff and Ticket – all are included, but you have to look elsewhere for the quaintly named 'One Engine in Steam' arrangements, which I had at one station. The later Track Circuit Block, as well as working over single lines using, for example, the electric token, are described, together with the regulations to be observed.

Bell signals, so well known for so many years, are listed, as well as the working of signals and the block indicators. Of great importance, of course, was the use of emergency bell signals, such as 'Obstruction Danger', and what to do in the event of block equipment failure, telephone failure and, possibly, a requirement for Pilotman working.

The Signalmen's General Instructions state clearly that no unauthorised person is allowed in the signal box. Other general items include dealing with signal light failure, train regulation, use of lever collars, defective points and signals and, of course, arrangements during fog and falling snow, including sending for the fogsignalmen when the fog marking point is obscured. Use of telephones and sealed releases are described. Automatic half-barrier level crossing arrangements made an appearance in later times. Clocks must be checked daily between the hours of 9.00am and 10.00am.

Supplementary Notice of Signalling and Permanent Way Alterations

These were published when required and gave the date and place where resignalling and track layout alterations were to be implemented. They also included a diagram and details of the types of block that would apply.

Sectional Appendix to the Working Timetable and Books of Rules and Regulations

The Sectional Appendix books were interesting and each covered part of a BR Region. They showed such details as standard speed restrictions, for example on single lines when passing through connections at loops, maximum speeds for light engines, and loco horn codes. Such items were standard, but there were variations shown in the Sections that followed. Sections on different lines contained much detail. For example, the

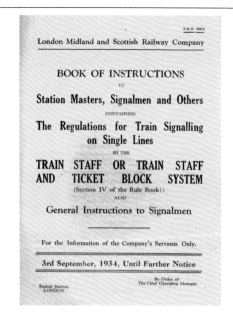

Above LMS Book of Instructions regarding the working of single lines, 1934. *WA*

Below Llanymynech, on the Central Wales Line, represents very much the sort of layout that came under the control of SMs in former times, and is an example of a junction of two single lines. Semaphore signals and manually operated points are in use, and signal wires and point rodding are everywhere. No 46516 brings the 1.30pm (SX) Llanfyllin to Oswestry train off the branch (to the right in the distance) on 27 June 1960; the branch opened in 1863 and closed completely in 1965.

11

SECTION B

TEMPORARY ENGINEERING WORKS

Materials may be lying about. Points and signals, etc. may be disconnected.

At or between	Lines affected	Remarks
MARYLEBONE TO DUNFORD BRIDGE (VIA HIGH WYCOMBE)		
London Midland Region (Western Lines)—		
Until further notice		
Wembley Hill	Down and up platforms	Demolishing station buildings. Ladders in use. Machine working.
Akeman Street and Grendon Underwood Jn.	All	07 00 to 17 00. Erecting scaffolding alongside track. 161 and 160 m.p.
Calvert and Culworth Jn.	Down and up	07 30 to 18 30. Contractors laying pipes under track between Calvert and Finmere, 156½ and 156¼ m.p. Machines working.
Rugby Central	Up loop and sidings	07 00 to 17 00. Removing track. Machines in use.
London Midland Region (Midland Lines):—		
Until further notice		
Loughborough Central and East Leake	Down and up	07 30 to 19 30. Contractors erecting and dismantling scaffolding and drawing overhead power lines across tracks, 92 and 91½ m.p. Boxes open as required.
New Basford and Bulwell Common North Jn.	All	08 00 to 18 00. Contractors painting bridges 272 to 280, 75¼ and 78 m.p.
New Hucknall Sidings and Holmewood Colliery (E.R.)	Down and up	Constructing new motorway structure 294, 64¾ and 64½ m.p. Temporary occupation crossing; protected under Rule 217A, in use by contractors.
Eastern Region—G.N. Lines:—		
Until further notice		
Heath Jn. and Duckmanton South Jn.	Down and up main	08 00 to 17 00. Erection of overhead cables, 57½ m.p. Scaffolding in use. Contractors on site.

A page from a London Midland Region booklet of supplementary instructions for the week 20-26 August 1966, showing temporary engineering works affecting the up and down lines between Loughborough and East Leake in connection with overhead power lines. East Leake station was unstaffed by this time. WA

King's Cross to Doncaster section has all the stations and signal boxes in route order with distances between each and the type of block in use. Even tunnels are shown, with their lengths but not the mileage from King's Cross. Additional lines, loops and refuge sidings, permanent speed restrictions, locations of catch points, spring or unworked trailing points, gradients and local horn codes then appear. These Sections constitute the main part of the book.

There then followed many lists of locations within the Sections where particular methods of working applied. Sometimes full standard instructions on how to carry out these methods were given, while in other cases you were referred to, say, the General Appendix, of which more later. The lists include locations where propelling of trains, working of freight trains without brake-vans and locos assisting in rear of trains were authorised.

Other items of interest include instructions for working down inclines, ie the pinning down and releasing of wagon brakes; level crossings opened and closed by trainmen, and open level crossings without gates or barriers; locations that had the greatest risk of lineside fires, particularly due to woods and plantations near the line; the towing of wagons in goods yards and sidings; electric bells and indicators for starting trains at stations; lines equipped with the Automatic Warning System (AWS); station yard working, for example whether more than one train at a time was allowed at the same platform; DMU tail traffic, for example parcels vans attached to a diesel unit; and the working of Officers' Specials, including maximum speeds when being propelled.

There are many more lists including standard head lamp or disc codes and details about various types of train heating, as well as instructions that excursions and special trains must carry the train number as shown in the Special Traffic Notice (STN) on the front of the loco and on the rear coach by means of a tablet (or a label could be used on the coach).

The workings of weedkilling trains and breakdown trains are shown, with the maximum speeds to be observed. Instructions about re-railing diesel locos and the coupling and uncoupling of locos follow, then arrangements for snow ploughs, steam lances, ground frames released from signal boxes and the crank handle operation of points.

LOCAL INSTRUCTIONS
ST. PANCRAS

Telephones are provided at the up fast home 2 and the up goods home signals and when light engines are detained at these signals, Drivers must immediately communicate with the Signalman, by telephone, giving particulars of the train they are required to work or their next working.

WORKING OF LIGHT ENGINES AND PLATFORM LINES. Unless instructed by the Station Master to remain coupled to the train for steam heating purposes, engines of incoming trains must be detached as soon as they come to a stand, and unless instructed to the contrary, or where the engine is not required to bank the empty stock, Drivers must, when the train is again departing, follow at a safe distance as far as the home 1 (platform starting) signal (except No. 5 platform) but must not pass such signal until it has been placed to Danger and taken off again. In the case of No. 5 platform the engine must follow at a safe distance as far as the position light shunting signal reading along No. 5 platform or to siding 8.

PASSENGER AND EMPTY COACHING STOCK TRAINS ASSISTED BY AN ENGINE IN THE REAR. The first paragraph of Rule 133 (c) does not apply to passenger and empty coaching stock trains starting from St. Pancras, and which are assisted by an engine in the rear in accordance with the arrangements laid down in Table " J," and in such cases the Guard's signal to start the train must be given to the Driver of the train engine who, provided the fixed signal is off, must acknowledge the Guard's signal by a short whistle; the train engine and, provided the banking indicator is off, assisting engine may then move forward.

UNCOUPLING OF ENGINES OF PASSENGER AND EMPTY COACHING STOCK TRAINS ON Nos. 6 and 7 PLATFORM LINES. Referring to the instructions shown on page 318, the Fireman will, in the absence of a Shunter, perform the duty of uncoupling the engine from a passenger or empty coaching stock train in cases where it is necessary for the engine to return to Station box through the crossover road near the buffer stops.

ENGINES ENTERING THE NORTH END OF THE GOODS SHED AND SHUNTING OPERATIONS INSIDE THE SHED, ST. PANCRAS. An engine may proceed its own length in the goods shed on any line to allow for the points being closed, and on " Waring's " road, as far as necessary to deal with four wagons in the loco. coal road. When in the goods shed engines must be worked very lightly, with the damper shut.

The Yard Inspector, or person appointed by him, must examine the shed after an engine has been working in it.

Shunting operations inside the shed must be performed from that side of the wagons where there are no columns supporting the upper stories of the shed.

Coupling and uncoupling of wagons in the spaces between the roads where there are supporting columns is strictly prohibited.

TELEPHONE COMMUNICATION BETWEEN TURNTABLE SIDING AND OLD LOCO. SIDINGS AND ST. PANCRAS STATION BOX. Telephone communication is provided at the North and South ends of the prime turntable siding and also at the old loco. sidings to enable Enginemen to communicate with the Signalmen at St. Pancras Station box.

When an engine is ready to leave the turntable sidings or old loco. sidings, the Fireman must inform the Signalman at St. Pancras Station box, by means of telephone, the train his engine is booked to work, and whether the engine is standing first, second or third from the exit.

SOMERS TOWN GOODS DEPOT

A loud sounding electric bell is fixed alongside the departure line from Somers Town Goods Depot to warn Shunters and others when a train is about to enter the Depot on the departure line. The bell will continue to ring until the movement has come to a stand.

No six-wheeled vehicle should be allowed to pass through the slip between the arrival and departure lines in the Depot.

WORKING OF TRAFFIC BETWEEN NORTH LONDON INCLINE BOX AND SOMERS TOWN COAL DEPOT. Before a train is allowed to enter these sidings it must be brought to a stand at the North London Incline box up home signal, and the Guard must ascertain that all the points are in the proper position, and that the line on which the train is to enter the sidings is clear.

KENTISH TOWN

SHUNTING ON DOWN GOODS LINE IN CAMDEN ROAD TUNNEL. A white marker light is provided about 230 yards from the St. Paul's Road Goods Junction end of the tunnel which must not be passed by Drivers of shunting movements proceeding under the authority of the shunt ahead signal along the down goods line. A mechanical point is fixed about 50 yards in rear of the light to indicate to Drivers their position in the tunnel.

The down goods line starting signal for St. Paul's Road Goods Junction box will be used for shunting movements when the line is clear to the Islip Street Junction down goods home signal, and Drivers of shunting movements proceeding under the authority of this starting signal may pass the white marker light in the tunnel as may be necessary.

A loud sounding electric bell fixed at the North end of Kentish Town Road Overbridge is in use to warn men at work on the line when a train is about to set back from Kentish Town Station or any point south of the crossover road.

337

The first page of the Local Instructions in the BR (LMR) Sectional Appendix to Working Timetable and books of Rules and Regulations *dated 1 October 1960. The book runs to 385 pages. The title page states, 'Employees supplied with this book must make themselves acquainted with it and will be held responsible for the observance of all instructions contained therein so far as they concern them.' WA*

To conclude this part there are many details about lamps: tail and side lamp repairs, Bardic lamps, defective signals, Tilley and warning board lamps. Point heater instructions follow. No list of this type would be complete without reference to clocks and watches: when clocks were sent for repairs the pendulum must be detached and securely fastened to the side of the clock. Watches were issued to guards and must be looked after.

Local Instructions constituted the final part of the Sectional Appendix. An SM was, of course, mainly concerned with his own local details, but also those for locations where his staff might work and other people's staff when working in his area. The SM needed to know these instructions and ensure that they were complied with. They showed what you were authorised to do, methods of working often being unique to a particular place, and, of course, the safety elements. These covered BR staff working in the vicinity and often customers' staff as well.

An example is shown in the details for the Maltings at Dereham. A red flag by day and a red light during darkness had to be placed by the firm's staff on the second storey of the Maltings, to warn shunters that people were loading and unloading wagons in the sidings; the greatest care had to be taken when shunting under these circumstances. Rule 112 of the Rule Book amplified this instruction.

The Great Yarmouth Tramway system has an entry in the Sectional Appendix. It is mainly to do with the speed restrictions to be observed and the requirement for each train to be preceded by a man with a red flag by day or red lamp after dark. He should be about 10 yards ahead of the loco or, if the train is being propelled, ahead of the foremost wagon. The maximum speed is 6mph, but 4mph through facing points and only 2mph near Haven Bridge. This system served the quayside, riverside properties, fish wharf, Beach station, coal sidings and yards, and the driver worked under the instructions from the shunter. Traffic carried included fish, coal, timber and insulated containers. In steam days Class 'J70' tram locos and the double-ended Class 'Y10' locos (originally used on the Wisbech & Upwell Tramway) were in regular use; diesels arrived in 1952 and the whole system closed at the end of 1975.

There is an interesting reference to an

'Open and Shut' lever situated at Ely North Junction. The lever was worked by the guard or shunter requiring to shunt a train into the down refuge sidings, and it operated an indicator in the signal box showing 'Open Points' or 'Shut Points'. When the train was clear of the points the lever was returned to the 'Shut Points' position.

To demonstrate the sheer diversity of entries in the Local Instructions I should like to mention details entitled 'Humber Ferry – Emergency Arrangements'. If the ferry boats could not sail due to fog or other circumstances, a telegram must be sent to the Divisional Manager and a large number of stations, and the code word 'Fog' should be used. A telegram using the word 'Clear' was sent to advise resumption of normal working. Passengers, of course, were to be kept fully informed of the situation.

The Sectional Appendix from which the accompanying examples of content are taken contains a brief description of the four examples of this type of three-position semaphore signal in the locality of Keadby, Lincolnshire. This one is showing Caution as No 90024 heads away from Althorpe station on 6 April 1964.

There are also details about Woodhead Tunnel regarding examination of the line, the telephone system in the tunnel and full instructions about protection of trains and requesting assistance in the event of a train coming to a stand in the tunnel.

At a nearby colliery guards detaching loaded wagons must take one label from each wagon and record the time and date of arrival, then they were to be handed to the signalman.

There are some details about the three-position semaphore signals situated at Gunhouse Junction and Keadby Canal Junction; these were unusual in that Danger was indicated by the signal arm being horizontal, at Caution the arm was at an angle of 45 degrees upper quadrant, and the Clear position was vertical.

From time to time there was a supplement to the Sectional Appendix showing amendments.

Rule Book, 1950

This Rule Book superseded the pre-nationalisation companies' own books, and is one of the first books that anyone connected with the railways would think of in connection with Rules & Regs and Safety of the Line.

We have already seen a little of it

regarding the particular rules applicable directly to the SM, but many other staff had to learn their relevant sections, and just a brief look at the batches of rules (rather than chapters as such) indicates that some parts were quite specific to signalmen, shunters and Engineer's staff.

The first section is, in fact, entitled 'General' and is very much to do with people employed by the railway and what is expected of them, for example attendance at medical exams, absence from duty conditions, conduct of staff, etc. Although this is a staff or personnel part of the book, the longest single rule is entirely to do with safe shunting procedures. It is good to see that Rule 2 states that 'Employees MUST ... see that the safety of the public is their chief care under all circumstances'. While the first part of the 1926 LNER Rule Book is very similar in many ways, there is a change from 'railway servant' in those days to 'railway employee' later. Another notable change is that there is no longer a problem with staff on duty or in uniform entering the station Refreshment Room without permission from the SM!

The second section is of interest as it is concerned with the control and working of stations. Every exertion must be made to ensure punctuality of trains, and when a train has completed its journey it must be searched and the windows closed. Doors of a departing train must be fastened before departure is allowed, and no passenger must join the train after that. Similarly, on arrival passengers must not alight before the train has come to a stand, and a warning must be given to any passenger trying to join or alight from a train that is in motion. A passenger train must not call at a station if not booked to do so unless there is special authority.

One rule concerns the working of cranes, including special steps to be taken if a running line will be obstructed by part of the crane working nearby. When a horse is used on the railway, a man must hold its head when a train is about to pass. There are also some interesting rules about privately owned locos: if under its own power the loco must not be allowed on any running line except when authorised by the Operating Superintendent, and if it is to be hauled in

The notice on the platform at Hull Paragon states 'Passengers must not enter or leave trains in motion', the subject of Rule 25.

a train, it must first be examined by the Motive Power or C&W Departments.

At terminal passenger stations, after sunset or during fog or falling snow, there must be a red light on the buffer stops on each line or on any train or vehicle standing there.

There follow sections about fixed signals, including drawings of them, and handsignals – an SM had to have a thorough knowledge of both. The handsignal instructions also include drawings and, on many occasions, I used these signals to give instructions to drivers. Normally they were in everyday use by shunters, guards, signalmen and firemen, while fogsignalmen and handsignalmen used them as required. For the most part, the hand signals were indications to drivers to make particular moves. One exception was the exchanging of signals between guard and fireman before a train departed. In many cases platform staff would also be involved in the train departure process, giving hand signals as appropriate.

Rules 55 and 56 were particularly well known to anyone involved in train running. Rule 55 was concerned with detention of trains on running lines. In particular, the signalman must be reminded about a train held at a stop signal: the driver must sound the engine whistle and, if still detained, the guard, shunter or fireman must go to the signal box and sign the Train Register Book. The signalman must also make use of lever collars or other appliances to serve as reminders that certain signals must not be cleared. Rule 56 goes on to give instructions if there is a block or telephone failure situation and a train is detained.

Further important sections follow. The use of detonators and the working of points and signals; disconnections of interlocking and signals for repair; and

how to deal with defective signals and other equipment are all items for which detailed rules applied. Then came the SM's and other people's responsibilities regarding signalling during fog and falling snow.

Level crossing rules follow, including how the gates should be operated and the use of signals if these were provided. There are instructions about lamps and what to do in the event of equipment being defective.

The shunting rules state that drivers must only work to signals given by the guard, shunter or other person in charge. Double shunting is described, when during one propelling movement some wagons would be put into one siding and others into another. 'Loose shunting' is where the wagons do not remain coupled to the loco. In both cases there are instructions about the duties of the shunting staff.

As one might expect there are strict rules about the checking of movements over facing points – the points must be fitting correctly – and wagons must be properly secured in a siding and not stand foul of adjoining lines.

Head, tail and side lamps merit a section of their own, while 'Working of Trains' is a section giving many instructions relevant to drivers, firemen and guards. One example is that the fire should be arranged so as to avoid unnecessary emission of smoke at stations and prevent blowing off steam as far as possible. There are also details about freight trains assisted in rear, light engines to be coupled together when required to pass through a block section at the same time, and the coupling together of two freight trains.

If a train was double-headed the driver and fireman of the leading loco were responsible for observance of signals, but the driver of the second loco also had

Above No 45063 is at Cardigan Road, Leeds, with the 11.35am Neville Hill-Cardigan Road 'trip' goods on 6 April 1964, and is 'loose shunting' at the coal drops, out of sight to the right. Rule 110 of the Rule Book gave instructions regarding this type of shunting.

Right Catch or trap points are the subject of several Rules. These trap points are open and the signal is at danger, so there is clear evidence of the cause of the derailment. In the background 'J39' No 64969 has charge of the breakdown train.

important duties. Another item is what action was to be taken if a train overran a station or stopped short of a platform. The situation regarding catch points or other spring points is detailed as regards trains moving over them or being brought to a stand on or near them. Trains were under the control of the guard.

Propelling of trains was only allowed under particular circumstances, and the Rule Book includes a list of 11 such items.

Smoking was not to be allowed in non-smoking compartments or coaches. If a passenger was drunk or disorderly the guard should attempt to deal with the problem, having the offender removed from the train if necessary. Unnecessary shunting where there were wagons of livestock involved was to be avoided.

Next there are extensive regulations

about trains stopped by accident, failure, obstruction or other exceptional cause. These include protection of the obstruction, train divided, and the issuing of Wrong Line Order forms. There were four types of these forms, each of a different colour, and I recall trying to memorise them, including who issued each and to whom they were addressed.

A well-known set of rules concerning single line working (SLW) – or, to give it the correct title, 'Working traffic of a double line over a single line of rails during repairs or obstruction – was appropriate as they explained clearly what SLW entailed. Certainly an SM would be involved at one time or another with these rules.

Finally there is a set of rules headed 'Permanent-way and Works' with details

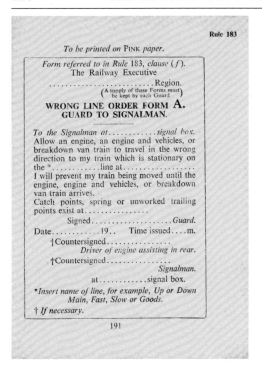

Rule 183

To be printed on PINK paper.

Form referred to in Rule 183, clause (f).
The Railway Executive
.........................Region.
(A supply of these Forms must be kept by each Guard)
WRONG LINE ORDER FORM A.
GUARD TO SIGNALMAN.

To the Signalman at...........signal box.
Allow an engine, an engine and vehicles, or
breakdown van train to travel in the wrong
direction to my train which is stationary on
the *...........line at................
I will prevent my train being moved until the
engine, engine and vehicles, or breakdown
van train arrives.
Catch points, spring or unworked trailing
points exist at................
Signed...................Guard.
Date...........19..   Time issued....m.
†Countersigned...............
Driver of engine assisting in rear.
†Countersigned...............
Signalman.
at...........signal box.
*Insert name of line, for example, Up or Down
Main, Fast, Slow or Goods.
† If necessary.

191

Wrong Line Order Form A: an example printed
in the Rule Book. This was the pink copy, issued
by the guard to the signalman. WA

for Engineer's staff, including the use of
trolleys and ballast train working;
relaying, repair and obstructions rules
covering the protection of lines; the use of
handsignalmen; and the introduction of
speed restrictions during repair work or,
indeed, for longer periods. The use of
speed restriction warning boards, together
with the commencement 'C' indicator
where the restriction actually starts and
the termination 'T' indicator, is described.

General Appendix to the Working Timetable and books of Rules and Regulations

As the title suggests, this book amplified
the instructions given in various books,
including the Rule Book. In addition
there were large sections giving detailed
descriptions and instructions about a wide
variety of items, including the air brake,

lighting of passenger trains and the
Automatic Warning System (AWS).

The first, short, part was about the Rule
Book, and among other things defined
'station limits', ie the portion of line
between the Home or Outer Home signal
and the section (Starting) signal worked
by a signal box – this section of line was
not part of the block section. There were
differences if Track Circuit Block was in
use, and Intermediate Block had its own
rule. In the next part the regulations for
the transmission of verbal messages are
shown, and the utmost importance of
making direct or telephone messages
perfectly clear is emphasised. Where
Safety of the Line was concerned there
must be no misunderstandings due to
imprecise wording.

Next came descriptions and regulations
for the working of the automatic air brake
on loco-operated trains, then the
automatic vacuum brake. The AWS is
explained, together with instructions
about its operation.

Several types of block working are next
described. These were the less well-
known systems, and the duties of the
relevant members of staff were shown.
Permissive Block was the system where
more than one train was permitted to be
in a block section at the same time, and
applied only where authorised. 'No Block
Regulations' was used in some cases where
trains worked over certain goods lines
where no block system applied. Four
systems were in use on single-line
railways: Electric Token working, Train
Staff and Ticket, One Train Working, and
Tokenless Block.

Details are shown concerning the
coupling together of either diesel or
electric locos, and the differences
between multiple working and tandem
working are described. Instructions for
working of DMUs follow, then
Freightliner and 'merry-go-round' (MGR)

Instructions for working diesel multiple units (DMUs) were introduced with this new form of train, and the transition from steam to diesel is well illustrated in this photograph at Leeds Central on 10 January 1957.

trains. Engineer's on-track self-propelled machines have a large set of instructions.

Permanent speed restriction signs are described in detail, as are the arrangements for detonators, including colour codes to denote the year of manufacture.

The equipment that a guard should have with him and the standard equipment held in a passenger or freight guard's van are specified. The standard code of head lamps or discs is shown, together with diagrams to show their positions on the front of the loco. There are instructions about flood conditions, for example at what level should normal working by diesel locos or DMUs cease.

Coupling, including loco to train or vehicles to each other, has a set of instructions, covering the use of screw couplings, instanter and buck-eye couplings. Wheel slip by locos or multiple units and the damage it can cause is described and there are appropriate instructions about this matter.

There is also a useful table showing how to calculate the speed of trains by the use of quarter-mile posts.

The lighting of passenger trains is, of course, an important item and there are the necessary instructions about steam heating, including the dates between which heating should be available each year. The actual operation of the equipment appeared in the Sectional Appendix.

Passenger trains must not be allowed to run on goods lines or goods loops except under special authority.

As can be seen, many of the foregoing were of relevance to the SM and he needed to be conversant with and ensure adherence to items concerning his area. Other items were also very relevant to the SM in most cases. For example, brake tenders, locos and brake vans coupled together, and instructions for descending inclines were important matters under the heading of 'Working of Freight Trains', as were details about the conveyance of out-of-gauge loads by ordinary train and coaching stock by freight train. An important section concerns how to deal with defective wagons, whether railway or privately owned.

Also shown are steps to be taken in the event of the line being blocked by accident or other obstruction and advice to passengers about delays due to this type of incident. Train divided, ramps for re-railing, and derailments in private sidings each have sets of instructions.

Returning to passenger station work, we have instructions about the whitening of platform edges and how to take precautions about barrows, trolleys and luggage on platforms. How to deal with lineside fires is an important item.

Then follows a list of duties for relevant staff when there is frost or snow. Snow ploughs, point heaters, signal boxes and level crossings to be kept open as necessary, and Permanent Way and S&T staff to be advised of requirements are all mentioned in the instructions in order to keep lines open and trains moving.

Under the heading of 'Miscellaneous', the following are of interest: 'Limited Clearance' boards, indicating restricted clearance between a running line or siding and an adjacent structure or between running lines and/or sidings; 'Whistle' boards; broken carriage windows; livestock in transit; homing pigeons; and standard railway sketching. The sketching details show how points, signals and many other items should be shown in reports in order to achieve uniformity.

Passenger Timetables of the 1960s

As well as the actual timetables there were references to bus-rail links and interavailability of tickets. Copies of the British Railways Board Bye-laws could be purchased in 1967 for half-a-crown (2s 6d). BR-appointed Travel Agents were listed, offering a wide range of tickets and information. Station car parks, car hire and the travel warrant scheme were also mentioned. Passengers Luggage in Advance (PLA) was an important feature at the time, while group travel, Railrover and Runabout tickets and availability conditions for ordinary and cheap tickets were shown.

Stations at which bath accommodation was available were shown in the North Eastern Region timetable for 1966 – this included Leeds City and Newcastle Central – and Motorail and Pullman

'Meals and Refreshments on Trains' from the Winter 1964 BR (LMR) Passenger Timetable. *WA*

services were also featured. Seat reservations and regulation tickets, sleeping cars and meal prices in restaurant cars complete a list of some of the main items in the Introduction to the public timetable of the day.

Passenger Working Timetable, 1960s

This book has an important first page emphasising how important are the railway's customers, whether passenger, parcels or freight, and how their requirements should be met. This was a timetable for use by railway staff. Times are shown to the half-minute and there are distances in miles and chains for stations and passing points. The four-digit train number appears at the head of each column and 'DMU' is shown where the train was booked to be a diesel multiple unit – this also applied in public timetables at one time.

Supplementary Operating Instructions

This book was issued periodically with amendments to several of the books mentioned above. In addition, miscellaneous items such as SMs being instructed to deal with any cases of occupation level crossings (a private road crossing the line) where gates were being left open; the re-designation of locos to become 'mixed traffic', for example the ex-LMS 'Jubilee' Class; and amendments to the numerical sorting system for parcels are followed by amendments to the route availability of locos, and there are also

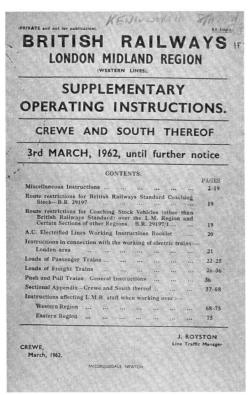

amendments to a booklet dated 1956 on the subject of the diversion of trains in case of accident or other emergency.

This is not a comprehensive list of the official publications that an SM had to know. There were considerable numbers of Rules & Regs, many having evolved over the years in numerous books before the BR versions appeared. Some of the rules had been effectively brought in by government legislation, particularly during the 19th century.

Of the books not described it would be worth mentioning the Working Manual for Rail Staff, Point to Point timings, and Route Availability books. It is difficult to draw a line between what could be described as Rules & Regs and other books that enabled staff to do their jobs. Further, the SM would need to be conversant with the Conditions of Carriage and the railway bye-laws. Certainly most of the books mentioned had one objective in mind: this was, of course, a safe railway for passengers, railway staff and everyone else involved.

Formal disciplinary procedures were in force during my time as an SM, and among other matters they might also be used in the case of infringements of Rules & Regs. The SM would be involved in the use of these procedures. Early disciplinary methods included a system of cautions, fines, etc, and were in use by the 1870s. Since the 1850s railway staff had been subject to medical examinations and were expected to be of good character.

It is interesting that, from the earliest days of the railways, military terminology was used, and this included the relationships between the SM and his staff. You worked in the service and reported for duty – if not, you might be regarded as being absent without leave – and holidays were called annual leave.

CONCLUSION

I would like to sum up by looking at the original and continuing purposes, up to 1970, of having an SM in charge of a station, and what he did. Perhaps half a dozen points – not in any order of priority – will suffice:

- To ensure that the requirements of passengers and those of parcels and goods customers were met – resulting in revenue being maximised.
- To ensure safety in all its aspects.
- To supervise the staff under his control.
- To ensure economic use of stores and equipment, and financial control generally.
- To ensure that the trains ran to time.
- To ensure that the station was well run, clean, tidy and welcoming.

We have seen, in some detail, how the SM did his job in order to meet these objectives, and this important work continued for more than 100 years. When Station and Area Managers came on to the scene in the 1960s and very early 1970s it was at a time when changes had already started as regards local management of stations. This was continued during periods of even greater change on the railways, as everywhere else in the modern world.

The station and line closures of the 1960s changed the situation, with many SMs' jobs disappearing and fewer opportunities of becoming an SM. Even without closures, the merging of jobs also had an effect with, say, three jobs being merged into one as at Castleford – although in that case there was an Assistant SM partly due to the number of signal boxes to be supervised. This merging of jobs poses the obvious questions of why it could not have been done earlier, and why nearly every station, at one time, had its own SM.

Looking at the situation of three types of station, small, medium and large, it is amazing nowadays to think just how much and what diversity of traffic there was even at small stations. In country areas huge amounts of agricultural traffic were dealt with, often very seasonal. Passengers continued to use small stations, but buses and, from the early 1960s perhaps, the car started to make a difference. When I began my career with BR in 1954, many small stations were still busy, while many medium and large stations continue to provide essential transport services to this day and see more and more passengers; happily this is also true of many of the smaller stations that survived and the new ones that have opened.

From the earliest days every station of any size would have boasted a full complement of staff under the Station Master, and no photographic opportunity was lost to emphasise the point. Here we see 'railway servants', clerical and manual, at Maghull on the Lancashire & Yorkshire Railway north of Liverpool, and at an unidentified location in the Manchester area. *Both John Ryan collection*

In 1958 the railway network was still largely intact, with stations large and small providing wide-ranging passenger and goods services. Above is Bartlow, with No 69651 and the 10.17am Haverhill-Audley End push-and-pull train on 11 April. It is standing at the very short Audley End branch platform, having earlier arrived chimney first at the main platform. Note the oil lamps and small wooden shelter for passenger use. Bartlow closed in 1967.

By contrast, the 30 July 1958 photograph shows Ashford (Kent), a main-line station still very much alive today, and associated with continental traffic via the Channel Tunnel, which was still a distant dream 50 years ago.

Above The classic pre-Beeching railway scene. This is Yatton, with No 1409 waiting with the 3.35pm Yatton-Clevedon branch train on 2 August 1958. I was travelling on the late-running Bristol train in the background, and there was obviously time to take a photo of the Clevedon train as we were awaiting a connection off the Wells line. However, the guard of the Wells train, just arriving, shouted across to the inspector to say that there was nobody requiring a connection with the Bristol train. The 'right away' was therefore given, which was smart station work even if it did give your photographer a pretty quick sprint to board the train through the guard's door and away to Bristol!

Below Calverley & Rodley station, between Leeds and Skipton, closed in 1965. On 20 August 1966 the four-platform station is being demolished as No 70036 (formerly *Boadicea*) passes with the 9.25am (SO) Glasgow Central-St Pancras service. This was a period of decline in the number of SMs' jobs due to station closures.

However, I think there were two reasons why merging of jobs became possible and the need for an SM at nearly every station became a thing of the past. First, staff numbers came into the equation: these were reduced for many reasons, such as passengers paying their fares on the train instead of at a booking office; level crossings became automated; and signal boxes closed when new power boxes took over. There was also a reduction in shunting: some of the old types of goods traffic and methods used have disappeared, and while it is encouraging to see new traffics appearing, it is sad that the goods yards of yore are but a memory.

Second, modern methods of communication became an important feature as the 1960s progressed. Although the mobile phone and computers were in the future, the use of telephones at home and work, improved systems at work, and the car all brought changes that meant that the days of an SM living in the station house were coming to an end. He had been available when needed and quite often had daily jobs such as booking tickets, but this was all changing and larger areas could be covered effectively. Other, less obvious changes also made a difference: pay no longer had to be worked out using pencil and paper, and ticket issuing and freight paperwork were similarly being modernised.

On a slightly different subject, but very relevant, the SM had a good deal of day-to-day contact with his staff. During my time with BR there were systems known as Negotiation and Consultation, whereby an SM met representatives of the staff to discuss, in a formal manner and on a regular basis, such local matters as staff rosters and leave arrangements. Matters with longer-term effects might also be discussed.

Not long ago I visited a country station that I found to be as near to the traditional station as I have seen for a long time – from an appearance point of view, I should add. Somerleyton is situated on the Norwich to Lowestoft line. A pleasant though rather long lane from the charming village brought me to the station, which was relatively untouched. It was unstaffed but the platforms and semaphore signals reminded me of so many stations I once knew, although the signal box was some distance away instead of at the end of the platform. It is nice to know that quite a few stations continue to exhibit an 'old world charm' as well as providing an important transport role.

Today many railway jobs are advertised nationally. Station Managers' jobs sometimes cover groups of stations or a large station together with a few smaller ones. In one recent job advert for a Station Manager at a fair-sized station, the following were mentioned: customer service, people management, meeting budgets, and developing and implementing training plans. Not so different.

The policeman and station clerk of the very earliest days would not recognise much of today's world. However, a visit to a local station would reveal railway people still working hard, often at all hours of the day and night, continuing to provide an essential service.

INDEX

Tailpiece: No 31551 leaves Paddock Wood with the 5.50pm service to Hawkhurst on 28 April 1961.